CRIME, GUILT, AND
PUNISHMENT

CRIME, GUILT, AND PUNISHMENT

A Philosophical Introduction

C. L. TEN

CLARENDON PRESS · OXFORD

Oxford University Press, Walton Street, Oxford OX2 6DP
Oxford New York Toronto
Delhi Bombay Calcutta Madras Karachi
Petaling Jaya Singapore Hong Kong Tokyo
Nairobi Dar es Salaam Cape Town
Melbourne Auckland
and associated companies in
Berlin Ibadan

Oxford is a trade mark of Oxford University Press

Published in the United States
by Oxford University Press, New York

First published 1987
Reprinted 1989

British Library Cataloguing in Publication Data
Ten, C. L.
Crime, guilt, and punishment: a
philosophical introduction.
1. Punishment
I. Title
364.6'01   HV8675
ISBN 0-19-875082-X
ISBN 0-19-875081-1 Pbk

Library of Congress Cataloging in Publication Data
Ten, C. L.
Crime, guilt, and punishment.
Bibliography: p.
Includes index.
1. Punishment.   2. Criminal law.   3. Criminal justice,
Administration of.   I. Title.
HV8675.T44   1987   364.6   87-5571
ISBN 0-19-875082-X
ISBN 0-19-875081-1 (pbk.)

Printed in Great Britain
at the University Printing House, Oxford
by David Stanford
Printer to the University

FOR KIANG

PREFACE

THIS book is based on lectures given to first year philosophy students at Monash University. It is their continued interest which makes me think it worthwhile to develop the lectures for publication. Peter Singer read a very early version of Chapter 2 and gave me helpful comments. I also read parts of that chapter to a seminar in the Philosophy Department at the National University of Singapore, and received some useful comments. Most of Chapter 3 was read to a seminar in the Philosophy Department at Monash University, and I profited from the discussion, especially from points raised by Frank Jackson and Peter Singer. Conversations with Rusi Khan have helped me clarify some of the ideas in the book. John Finnis and Denis Galligan kindly made available to me some of their publications on punishment from which I have benefited. My greatest debt is to H. L. A. Hart. Even the numerous references in this book to his work do not fully reflect the extent of my debt. It was his seminal work on punishment which first aroused my interest in the subject and influenced my general approach as well as the details of many of my arguments. At very short notice he read through a draft of the book and saved me from a number of mistakes and stylistic infelicities. I am also very grateful to him for his constant encouragement and for many acts of kindness which he has shown me over the years. I am of course solely responsible for any remaining errors in the book. Monash University granted me leave in 1985 under its Outside Studies Programme and this was indispensable to the completion of the book. I am conscious of the sacrifices which my wife and daughter made to enable me to write under ideal conditions. Lesley Whitelaw and Lynette Carter efficiently typed up the final version of the manuscript amidst the numerous other demands on their time.

CONTENTS

1 INTRODUCTION   1

2 THE UTILITARIAN THEORY

2.1. The Effects of Punishment   7

2.2. Punishing the Innocent   13

2.3. Punishment and Guilt   14

2.4. The Disutility of Punishing the Innocent   17

2.5. Fantastic Examples and Moral Principles   18

2.6. Moral Dilemmas and Complexities   32

2.7. A Return to the Real World   36

3 RETRIBUTIVE THEORIES

3.1. Introduction   38

3.2. Punishment Annuls Crime   38

3.3. Nozick's Retributivism: Connecting with Correct Values   42

3.4. Punishment and Desert   46

3.5. Wrongdoers Deserve to Suffer   47

3.6. Unfair to Victims   49

3.7. Equality of Treatment Among Offenders   50

3.8. Punishment Gives Satisfactions   51

3.9. Unfairness to Law-Abiding Citizens   52

4 THE SCOPE AND WEIGHT OF REASONS FOR PUNISHMENT

4.1. Introduction   66

4.2. Rawls and Rule-Utilitarianism   67

4.3. The Scope and Weight of Retributive Theories   71

4.4. Hart's Theory   81

5 TREATMENT WITHOUT THE EXCUSES OF PUNISHMENT

5.1. Hart's Rationale of Legal Excuses   86

5.2. *Mens Rea*, Negligence, and Strict Liability   100

5.3. Wootton's System of Treatment   110

6 MENTALLY ILL OFFENDERS

   6.1. Legal Insanity   123

   6.2. The Abolition of the Insanity Defence?   128

   6.3. Dangerousness   134

7 THE AMOUNT OF PUNISHMENT

   7.1. Reducing Crime   141

   7.2. Just Deserts   150

   7.3. Sentencing   160

BIBLIOGRAPHY   165

INDEX   173

I

INTRODUCTION

OUR attention is often drawn to the manifestations and ramifications of crime and punishment. These are topics about which most people seem to have strong views, and many also have professional interests. Philosophers are among those who have debated issues about crime and punishment, and especially about the moral justification of punishment by the State. This is one area of philosophy which connects directly and obviously with the concerns of the general public. The problems of punishment are also related to other philosophical issues particularly in moral, legal, social, and political philosophy. For these reasons, a discussion of the nature and justification of punishment is a useful introduction to other related areas of philosophy, and to issues of interest to non-philosophers.

In this book, I offer such an introduction which begins mostly with rather abstract accounts of moral theories of punishment and the conflicts between them, and then proceeds to discuss some of the more practical implications of these theories. Punishment is a topic in which theory and practice should come together.

In what follows, I have not presupposed any knowledge of philosophy, or any other specialist knowledge. I have also not tried to give formal definitions of every technical term used, preferring instead to rely sometimes on the discussion and examples to make clear the sense of what is said. I have tried to indicate the connections between what is discussed and the broader issues relevant to the discussion. But I do not pursue these issues in great detail. To do so would risk losing the thread and continuity of my account of punishment. However, I hope that what I say, though brief, is sufficient to suggest the range of different issues which are linked to punishment. I do not write primarily for my fellow philosophers, but of course I hope that they too will find the book of some use, not least perhaps as illustrative of arguments they wish to reject, or of positions to be repudiated.

Punishment is administered not just by the State but also by others such as teachers and parents. My concern is with punishment by the State as imposed through the operation of the criminal law. Here there is a system of prohibitions and requirements whose violation leads eventually, after apprehension, a trial, and conviction, to some form of punishment. Of course quite often some of those who commit crimes escape punishment for a number of reasons: they are not apprehended, there is insufficient evidence to charge them, they are wrongly acquitted, etc. Sometimes too an innocent person may be wrongly convicted. But in the central cases of punishment, the person punished has committed the offence for which he or she is punished. It is a matter of dispute, into which we will be entering later, as to whether the notion of punishment can be extended to cover cases in which someone, known by the legal authority to be innocent, is made to pay a penalty in order to prevent some harm to the community. There is also the moral issue of whether we are ever justified in imposing a penalty in this way on an innocent person. Punishment is administered by the legal authority and not by a private individual or group in society. For example, it is not administered by the victim or the victim's friends or family. Punishment involves the infliction of some unpleasantness on the offender, or it deprives the offender of something valued. A fine deprives a person of his or her property, and imprisonment is a deprivation of freedom. They are very different from rewards which confer benefits on a person. Even a suspended sentence or a probation order is not something which the offender welcomes in itself, although of course it is preferred to the harsher forms of punishment. But punishment is not just the imposition of something unpleasant on the offender: the imposition is made to express disapproval or condemnation of the offender's conduct which is a breach of what is regarded as a desirable and obligatory standard of conduct. The importance of some of these features of punishment will emerge in the next chapter when we see their relevance in distinguishing punishment from other activities which appear to be very similar.[1]

[1] For useful discussions of the definition of punishment, see: Antony Flew, 'The

We are not normally justified in depriving people of the
things which they value, such as their liberty or their property.
So why is punishment justified? Philosophical theories of
punishment try to provide the moral basis for justifying punishment. But given that in any society there are at least some
criminal laws which are bad and should not have been enacted,
it is impossible for any theory of punishment to justify the
punishment of every person who is convicted of a criminal
offence. Theories of punishment specify the type of considerations which, if satisfied, will justify punishment. These
considerations are not always satisfied.

The philosophical debate on punishment has been dominated by two main types of theories of punishment, the
utilitarian theory and the retributive theory. The utilitarian
theory justifies punishment solely in terms of its beneficial
effects or consequences. It is in that sense a consequentialist
theory, sharing with all consequentialist theories the belief
that ultimately the only morally significant features of an act
are the good and bad consequences produced by it. A right
act is that which, among the available alternatives, produces
the best consequences.[2] Such an act is described as optimific.
Utilitarians are distinguished from other consequentialists by
their account of what constitutes the relevant consequences of
an act. They believe that the right act is that which produces
the greatest utility, or is most conducive to the welfare of all
those affected by the act. There are different accounts of utility
or welfare, and two such versions of utilitarianism have been
particularly prominent. The classical utilitarians, like Jeremy
Bentham, interpret utility or welfare in terms of the mental
state of happiness, and thus believe that the right or optimific
act is that which maximizes, or produces the most, happiness.
The second version of utilitarianism, popular among some
contemporary philosophers, thinks of the promotion of welfare

Justification of Punishment', in H. B. Acton (ed.), *The Philosophy of Punishment*
(London, 1969), pp. 83–7; H. L. A. Hart, *Punishment and Responsibility* (Oxford, 1968),
pp. 4–6; Joel Feinberg, 'The Expressive Function of Punishment', in Hyman Gross
and Andrew von Hirsh (eds.), *Sentencing* (New York & Oxford, 1981); and
Richard Wasserstrom, 'Capital Punishment as Punishment: Some Theoretical Issues
and Objections', in *Midwest Studies in Philosophy*, 7 (1982), pp. 475–8.

[2] More accurately, a right act is that which produces at least as good consequences
as all alternative acts, since two or more acts may produce equally good consequences.

in terms of maximizing the satisfaction of desires.[3] In the area
of punishment, the differences between these two versions of
utilitarianism do not generally bear on the issues that I shall
be discussing. Both see the main benefits of punishment in
terms of its contribution to the reduction of crime, and not in
terms of giving offenders what they deserve if what is deserved
is independent of, and conflicts with, the promotion of the
general welfare. So I concentrate here on the view of classical, or what is sometimes called hedonistic, utilitarianism.
Happiness is maximized by an act when the act produces the
greatest balance of pleasure over pain, or when it minimizes
pain if it should turn out that all available courses of action
each produces pain. So for the utilitarian, since punishment
is itself an unpleasant experience for the offender who is
punished, the infliction of punishment can only be justified if
it prevents greater suffering. It is never right to punish if the
good consequences of punishment are less than the suffering
caused by punishment.

Utilitarians believe that each person's happiness or welfare
counts for the same amount of happiness or welfare of another
person, and that it is possible to add up the individual amounts
into a total amount of general happiness or general welfare.
In choosing a course of conduct, one must therefore take into
account its effects on everyone, and consider the interests of
all impartially. The suffering of the wrongdoer, taken on its
own, makes no less a claim on us than the similar suffering
of the virtuous. But if this is so, then why should punishment
be confined to wrongdoers? Critics have argued that utilitarians are committed to punishing an innocent person if such
punishment maximises happiness. In Chapter 2, I consider
various utilitarian responses to this argument, and relate the
discussion to the more general issues of the role of examples
in moral argument and the nature of moral disagreements.

In their attitude towards the suffering of the wrongdoer
utilitarians disagree with retributivists, as those who subscribe to the retributive theory of punishment are called.

[3] For a brief account of some of the differences between these two versions of
utilitarianism, see C. L. Ten, *Mill on Liberty* (Oxford, 1980), pp. 4–5, 52–5. J. J. C.
Smart and Bernard Williams, *Utilitarianism: For and Against* (Cambridge, 1973) is a
useful general discussion of the disagreements between utilitarians and non-
utilitarians.

Retributivists regard the offender's wrongdoing as deserving of punishment, and the amount of punishment should be proportionate to the extent of the wrongdoing. The offender's desert, and not the beneficial consequences of punishment, is what justifies punishment. Retributivists differ in the details of their explanation of how punishment is supposed to give the moral wrongdoer what he or she deserves. Some of them regard the punishment of wrongdoers as derivative from a fundamental axiom of justice that wrongdoers deserve to suffer. Other retributivists try to connect punishment with broader issues of distributive justice, or justice in the distribution of the benefits and burdens of social life. The offender is viewed as someone who has taken an unfair advantage of others in society, and punishment restores fairness. These and other retributive justifications of punishment are discussed in Chapter 3.

Are retributive and utilitarian theories of punishment irreconcilable? They would be if retributivists insisted on punishing the wrongdoer irrespective of the consequences of such punishment, or if the utilitarian required that an innocent person should be punished whenever this would produce the best consequences. But attempts have been made to effect a compromise between them by, for example, confining their respective applications to different levels of conduct, or by reducing the weight to be attached to both retributive and utilitarian reasons for punishment so that each type of reason on its own would be insufficient to justify punishment. I examine compromise theories in Chapter 4.

It is an important feature of the practice of punishment that offenders are not punished simply because they have committed prohibited acts. The law recognizes various excuses like accident, duress, and reasonable mistake. Thus a person who deliberately kills is guilty of murder, but if the killing was purely accidental then the offender is not punished. In Chapter 5 I discuss the rationale of excuses, and consider whether there is an adequate utilitarian defence of legal excuses. The various excuses which exempt some offenders from punishment in spite of the social harm caused by their acts have been regarded by some as major hindrances to the prevention of socially harmful conduct. Thus Lady Wootton maintains that the only

reason why we retain excuses in the criminal law is in order
to confine punishment to the wicked, as those who cause harm
when they have an excuse are not wicked. But Wootton herself
rejects this view and sees the aim of the criminal law differently
as seeking to prevent socially harmful acts. Such acts are often
committed not by those who deliberately harm others, but by
those who, though not wicked, are serious social nuisances.
She recommends the abolition of legal excuses, and the replacement of punishment by a new system of treatment in which
persons are convicted if they have committed prohibited acts
irrespective of their mental states at the time, or of whether
they are morally culpable. Convicted offenders should be sentenced in accordance with what form of treatment would best
prevent them from repeating their harmful acts in future. I
critically examine Wootton's view in Chapter 5 and also in
Chapter 6 which is devoted to a discussion of mentally ill
offenders. The excuse of mental illness has generated much
controversy. I discuss some aspects of this controversy, and
examine the case for the protective sentencing of offenders
who are considered dangerous. Mentally ill offenders are often
included in this category.

Finally, even when it is agreed that a particular offender
should be punished, there is still the issue of the amount of
punishment to be meted out to him or her. In Chapter 7, I
examine utilitarian and retributive principles for determining
the appropriate degree of punishment, and make some brief
comments about sentencing practice.

I adopt a pluralist approach to punishment, believing that
in the practice of punishment we are often confronted with a
number of different considerations, each not reducible to the
others, and each having a contribution to make. My main
target therefore is any theory of punishment, whether it be
utilitarian or retributive, which seeks to justify punishment in
terms of just one ultimate value. At the same time I think that
both these types of theories embody valuable insights, and I
try to show how these can be accommodated within a pluralist
approach.

2

THE UTILITARIAN THEORY

2.1. *The Effects of Punishment*

THE utilitarian theory justifies punishment solely in terms of the good consequences produced. There are disagreements among utilitarians about the nature of the good consequences which punishment is supposed to produce. Some utilitarians may even believe that the harm done by punishment outweighs the good, and hence punishment is not justified. But many utilitarians see the main beneficial effects of punishment in terms of the reduction of crime, and believe that punishing offenders will have at least some, if not all, of the following good effects. First, punishment acts as a deterrent to crime. The deterrent effects can be both individual and general. Punishment deters the offender who is punished from committing similar offences in future, and it also deters potential offenders. The offender who is punished is supposed to be deterred by his experience of punishment and the threat of being punished again if he re-offends and is convicted. This is the individual deterrent effect. The general deterrent effect of punishment on potential offenders works through the threat of their being subjected to the same kind of punishment that was meted out to the convicted offender.

Secondly, punishment is supposed to have reformative or rehabilitative effects.[1] This is confined to the offender who is punished. He is reformed in the sense that the effect of

---

[1] Jack P. Gibbs distinguishes between 'rehabilitation' and 'reformation'. An offender is 'rehabilitated' if he ceases to violate the law as a result of non-punitive means, whereas he is 'reformed' if he ceases to violate the law as a result of punishment, but for reasons independent of the fear of punishment. See *Crime, Punishment, and Deterrence* (New York, 1975), p. 72. I use the two terms interchangeably and broadly to refer to cases in which the offender, after serving a sentence, no longer commits crimes because he believes that criminal behaviour is wrong and not because he fears punishment. His changed values can be brought about by punishment itself or by non-punitive means. Jean Hampton develops a sophisticated version of the moral education

punishment is to change his values so that he will not commit similar offences in future because he believes such offences to be wrong. But if he abstains from criminal acts simply because he is afraid of being caught and punished again, then he is deterred rather than reformed and rehabilitated by punishment. So the effects of individual deterrence and rehabilitation are the same. What distinguishes them is the difference in motivation.

The third good consequence of punishment is its incapacitative effect. When an offender is serving his sentence in prison, he is taken out of general social circulation and is therefore prevented from committing a variety of offences, even though he may neither be deterred nor reformed by punishment. Of course punishment would not have an overall incapacitative effect if the offender would not have re-offended even if he were free, or if his incarceration led someone else, who would not otherwise have done so, to engage in criminal activity, perhaps as his replacement in a gang. While in prison, the offender might still commit certain offences: he might assault a fellow prisoner or a prison guard. But his opportunities are generally reduced. In some cases, however, his contacts with other prisoners would create opportunities for further involvement in crime when he is released. The incapacitative effect, though perhaps most likely in the case of imprisonment, may also be present in other forms of punishment. For example, parole may have some incapacitative effect in that although the offender is free, the fact that he is under supervision may restrict his opportunities for criminal activities.

The empirical evidence of the effects of punishment is very complex, but a brief survey will be of some use.

It looks as if the present state of our knowledge provides no basis for claiming that punishment by imprisonment reforms or rehabilitates the criminal, or that it is an individual deterrent. The position is well summed up by the Report of the

view of punishment according to which punishment communicates a moral message aimed at educating both the wrongdoer and the rest of society about the immorality of the offence. She is eager to distinguish her view from rehabilitative theories of punishment both in terms of the different ends to be achieved and the methods used to attain those ends. According to her, the aim of rehabilitation is to make the offender accept society's mores and operate successfully in society, and the pursuit of these goals is not constrained by respect for the autonomy of the wrongdoer. See 'The Moral Education Theory of Punishment', *Philosophy & Public Affairs*, 13 (1984).

Panel of the National Research Council in the United States on Research on Deterrent and Incapacitative Effects, hereafter referred to as the Panel:

The available research on the impact of various treatment strategies both in and out of prison seems to indicate that, after controlling for initial selection differences, there are generally no statistically significant differences between the subsequent recidivism of offenders, regardless of the form of 'treatment'. This suggests that neither rehabilitative nor criminogenic effects operate very strongly. Therefore, at an aggregate level, these confounding effects are probably safely ignored.[2]

By 'criminogenic effects' the Panel refers to the undesirable effects of imprisonment in either increasing the criminal's propensity to commit crimes or to extend the duration of his criminal career. Such effects are the opposite of the rehabilitative effects. So the present evidence seems to suggest that in general the effect of imprisonment, or of the various programmes for rehabilitation which accompany imprisonment, is neither to make the criminal a better nor a worse person with respect to the standards of behaviour set by the criminal law.

The evidence also suggests that in general punishment has no individual deterrent effect. Daniel Nagin points out that at the observational level it is difficult to distinguish between individual (or what he calls special) deterrence and rehabilitation. He concludes that, 'The figures suggest that recidivism rates cannot be affected by varying the severity of the punishment, at least within acceptable limits.'[3] But Nagin cautiously adds that the evidence is only preliminary.

In a few specific cases there is indeed some evidence of the individual deterrent effect of punishment. Thus Johannes Andenaes draws attention to a study of amateur shoplifters which shows that detection and arrest, even without prosecution, produces serious shock. There is little or no recidivism among those who are apprehended and interrogated by the

[2] Alfred Blumstein, Jacqueline Cohen, and Daniel Nagin (eds), *Deterrence and Incapacitation: Estimating the Effects of Criminal Sanctions on Crime Rates*, National Academy of Sciences, Panel on Research on Deterrent and Incapacitative Effects (Washington, 1978), p. 66. Hereafter this book will be referred to as *The Panel*.

[3] Daniel Nagin, 'General Deterrence: A Review of the Empirical Evidence', in *The Panel*, p. 96.

store police and then set free without being formally charged.[4] A study of drunk driving in Sweden also shows that those drivers who had been arrested estimated the risk of being arrested as many times higher than other drivers.[5]

There is disagreement about the general deterrent effects of punishment. Johannes Andenaes believes that, 'In general terms it can only be stated that general deterrence works well in some fields and works poorly or not at all in other fields.'[6] But in 1974 Gordon Tullock published an article, 'Does Punishment Deter Crime?', in which he surveyed the work done by economists and sociologists.[7] Tullock points out that economists began their work under the impression that punishment would deter crime because demand curves slope downwards showing that if the cost of a good is increased then less of it will be consumed. So if the cost of committing crime is increased by more severe punishment, then there will be fewer crimes. Sociologists, on the other hand, started out with the intention of confirming what was then the accepted view in their discipline that punishment would not deter crime. But Tullock argues that, although their starting points and assumptions were radically different, both economists and sociologists, after analysing the evidence, came to the same conclusion that punishment did indeed deter crime. After surveying their studies Tullock himself is convinced that 'the empirical evidence is clear', and he states his conclusion unequivocally: 'Even granting the fact that most potential criminals have only a rough idea as to the frequency and severity of punishment, multiple regression studies show that increasing the frequency or severity of the punishment does reduce the likelihood that a given crime will be committed.'[8]

However, Tullock's confidence about the clarity of the empirical evidence is not shared by the Panel. The Panel argues that although the evidence consistently establishes a negative association between crime rates and sanctions (as

[4] Johannes Andenaes, 'Does Punishment Deter Crime?', in Gertrude Ezorsky (ed.), *Philosophical Perspectives on Punishment* (Albany, 1972), p. 354.

[5] Ibid., p. 354.

[6] Ibid., p. 346.

[7] Gordon Tullcock, 'Does Punishment Deter Crime?', *The Public Interest* (1974), pp. 103–11.

[8] Ibid., p. 109.

measured by the risks of apprehension, conviction, or imprisonment), that is higher crime rates are associated with lower sanctions and vice versa, this does not necessarily show the general deterrent effect of sanctions. The negative association may be partly or wholly explained in terms of lower sanctions being the effect rather than the cause of higher crime rates. Higher crime rates may so overburden the resources of the criminal justice system that they reduce its ability to deal with new offenders. Overburdened judges and prosecuters may use their discretion to dismiss or reduce charges, or to offer attractive plea bargains.[9] Overcrowding of prisons may lead to a reduction in the time served in prison as more prisoners are released early on parole. The sanctions imposed on certain crimes may be reduced. So unless one can separate out the effect of higher crime rates on sanctions from the deterrent effect of sanctions on crime, one cannot interpret the evidence as establishing the presence of the general deterrent effect of punishment. The Panel's cautious assessment of the evidence is summed up in its remark that 'we cannot yet assert that the evidence warrants an affirmative conclusion regarding deterrence', but the Panel adds that 'the evidence certainly favours a proposition supporting deterrence more than it favours one asserting that deterrence is absent'.[10] On the other hand, the Panel believes that the evidence does not even show a significant negative association between crime rates and the severity of punishment as measured by the time served in prison, but suggests that this may partly be accounted for in terms of various distortions.[11]

Moving from the analysis of statistics to the experimental evidence, the Panel identifies three studies which are not methodologically flawed. Of these, two show that the level of crime decreased significantly with increases in the level of sanctions, while one showed that the removal of criminal sanctions for abortions in Hawaii did not affect the incidence of abortions.[12] So it looks as if the present experimental evidence does not permit the drawing of general conclusions. But much

---

[9] *The Panel*, p. 39.
[10] Ibid., p. 7.
[11] Ibid., pp. 37–8.
[12] Ibid., p. 55.

of the experimental evidence is consistent with the operation of deterrence, as has been noted by Nigel Walker.[13]

Finally, we turn to the incapacitative effect of punishment. In her review of the literature for the Panel, Jacqueline Cohen suggests that disagreements about the magnitude of that effect can be attributed almost entirely to the different estimates of the average crime rate of prisoners.[14] The estimate of the increase in crime if current prison use were reduced or eliminated has been as low as five per cent.[15] Estimating the incapacitative effect of present prison policies is one thing. There is also the different question as to what we can expect the incapacitative effect to be if present policies are changed. Here one estimate is of a five fold decrease in crime, but Cohen points out that this can only be achieved by increasing the prison population by between 355 per cent and 567 per cent.[16] The incapacitative effect will not be the same for all crimes. Cohen points out that using the assumptions made by the available models, the increase in prison population required to reduce violent crimes is much less than the increases needed for similar reductions in other crimes. Violent crimes can be reduced by 10 per cent with less than 30 per cent increase in prison population.[17] This kind of consideration has led to an increasing interest in the use of selective incapacitation in which the focus of imprisonment is on certain types of offenders who are identified as having a high rate of committing crimes.[18]

We see that the evidence is perhaps more hospitable to the claim that punishment has some general deterrent effect and some incapacitative effect than it is to the claim that it has individual deterrent effect or that it rehabilitates offenders. This will no doubt be puzzling to some, but it provides a basis for caution in responding to a high rate of recidivism. Where there is such a high rate, it shows that punishment does not

---

[13] Nigel Walker, *Punishment, Danger and Stigma* (Oxford, 1980), pp. 77–80.

[14] Jacqueline Cohen, 'The Incapacitative Effect of Imprisonment: A Critical Review of the Literature', in *The Panel*, p. 209.

[15] Ibid., p. 188.

[16] Ibid., p. 218.

[17] Ibid., p. 227.

[18] See Mark H. Moore, Susan R. Estrich, Daniel McGillis, and William Spelman, *Dangerous Offenders: The Elusive Target of Justice* (Cambridge, 1984). I discuss the problem of dangerous offenders in Ch. 6.

deter those who are punished. But it does not show that potential offenders are not in fact deterred by punishment, or that punishment does not incapacitate.

2.2. *Punishing the Innocent*

Let us now assume that the beneficial consequences of punishment outweigh the suffering that it inflicts on offenders. Critics of the utilitarian theory argue that if punishment is to be justified solely in terms of its good consequences, then punishment cannot be confined to offenders. There might be situations in which punishing an innocent person would produce better consequences that alternative courses of action. The utilitarian is therefore committed to punishing the innocent person. This objection has played an important role in the rejection of the utilitarian theory.

Let us consider an example made famous in the literature by H. J. McCloskey.[19] Suppose that in a particular town with a mixed population a man from one racial group rapes a woman from the other group. Because of existing racial tensions the crime is likely to produce racial violence with many people being injured, unless the guilty man is apprehended quickly. Suppose further that the sheriff of the town can prevent the violence by framing an innocent man who was near the scene of the crime, and who will be accepted by the community as the guilty person. Surely, it is argued, the best consequences will be produced by the sheriff's fabrication of evidence against him which will result in his conviction and severe punishment. But the critics maintain that the sheriff's act and the subsequent punishment of the innocent man are both wrong.

There are many ways in which utilitarians, or those sympathetic to them, can respond to this objection, and I shall consider some of their main arguments. First, it is argued that 'punishing the innocent' is a logical contradiction because punishment implies guilt. Secondly, the premises of the objection are challenged. It is suggested that punishing the innocent man will not in fact produce the best consequences if we take

[19] See H. J. McCloskey, 'A Non-utilitarian Approach to Punishment', in Michael D., Bayles (ed.), *Contemporary Utilitarianism* (New York, 1968). Some of the details of my example in the text differ from McCloskey's examples.

into account all the consequences of such punishment including the long-term and less obvious consequences. Thirdly, it
is claimed that the only situations in which punishing the
innocent is optimific are hypothetical and 'fantastic' situations
rather than situations which arise, or are likely to occur, in
the real world. It is then argued that for a variety of reasons,
utilitarians should not be worried by what they are committed
to in such fantastic situations. In discussing this third response,
I shall also consider the views of those utilitarians who maintain that the punishment of the innocent would indeed be
justified in situations where it produces the best consequences.
If 'commonsense morality' or our intuitions disagree, so much
the worse for them.

2.3. *Punishment and Guilt*

In his well-known paper, 'On Punishment', Anthony Quinton
argues that the notion of 'punishment' implies guilt in the
sense that 'punishment' is defined in part as the infliction of
suffering on the guilty.[20] So when suffering is inflicted on innocent people, this cannot be properly described as punishment
but as something else—judicial terrorism or social surgery. If
we inflict suffering on an innocent man and try to pass it off
as punishment, we are guilty of lying since we make a lying
imputation that he is guilty and responsible for an offence.
Part of Quinton's argument seems to rest on the importance
of distinguishing between, for example, typhoid carriers and
criminals even though both may sometimes be treated in rather
similar ways. Thus a typhoid carrier, or a person with an
infectious disease, will be quarantined. He will lose his freedom in much the same way that a criminal is deprived of his
freedom when he is jailed. And yet we do not call quarantine
a form of punishment precisely because the disease carrier is
not guilty of an offence.

It is certainly true that in the typical cases of punishment
it is inflicted on a person guilty of an offence. But the crucial
issue is whether we can extend the notion of punishment to
the infliction of suffering on the innocent without at the same
time losing the distinction between punishment and various

[20] Anthony M. Quinton, 'On Punishment', in H. B. Acton (ed.), *The Philosophy of
Punishment* (London, 1969), pp. 58–9.

activities like the quarantine of disease carriers and certain kinds of medical or dental treatment which are painful.

In all these cases there is the infliction of some unpleasantness or suffering, but it is only in the case of punishment that the unpleasantness is essential to what is to be done. As Wasserstrom puts it 'the point of the imposition of a deprivation when it is unmistakably a punishment is that it is being imposed because it is a deprivation, because the person upon whom it is being imposed should thereby be made to suffer and in that respect be worse off than before'.[21] On the other hand, the unpleasantness experienced by those who are quarantined, or by those undergoing medical treatment, is only incidental, and not essential to what needs to be done. Advances in medical technology may lead to the replacement of painful forms of treatment by pleasant, but still effective, treatment. Medical treatment does not have to be painful at all: a sweet pill is as much a medicine as a bitter pill. Similarly, quarantine implies a degree of isolation to prevent the spread of the infection, and that in itself will be unpleasant. But it can, if resources permit, be greatly outweighed by the pleasures of the surroundings in which one is put. But punishment implies at least an overall degree of unpleasantness. So we can distinguish between punishment and quarantine without falling back on the notion that the person who is punished must be guilty, or must at least be supposed to be guilty, of an offence.

However, the truth of the matter seems to be a bit more complex than we have so far acknowledged, and Quinton's argument, though mistaken, is interesting because it gestures towards that truth. Consider the difference between a monetary fine, which is a form of punishment, and a tax which is not. Arguably both are essentially unpleasant although both may be accepted or approved of as fully justified. What then is the difference between them? In *The Concept of Law* H. L. A. Hart points out that punishment involves 'an offence or breach of duty in the form of violation of a rule set up to

[21] Richard A. Wasserstrom, 'Capital Punishment as Punishment: Some Theoretical Issues and Objections', *Midwest Studies in Philosophy*, 7 (1982), p. 476. See also H. J. McCloskey, 'The Complexity of the Concepts of Punishment', *Philosophy*, 37 (1962), p. 323.

guide the conduct of ordinary citizens'.[22] When someone is punished, he has violated a standard of conduct to which he is supposed to conform. But when he pays a tax, he has not breached any such standard of conduct. The main purpose of taxes is to raise revenue and not to set up a standard of correct conduct. Indeed the revenue-raising function of a tax would be defeated if people generally reacted to income tax by not working, or to Value Added Tax by not eating in restaurants. On the other hand, the purpose of punishment is not defeated if, as a result of it, people cease to breach the relevant standard of conduct. On the contrary, the threat of punishment is most effective when it is unnecessary to carry it out. This important difference between punishment and a tax can be blurred, as Hart acknowledges, when, for example, those running a business simply assimilate the relatively small fines for breaches of rules into the costs of the goods they produce, and pass them on to their consumers. It is also blurred in the other direction when a government imposes a tax on luxury goods partly in order to discourage their use.

A related difference between punishment and other forms of deprivation or unpleasant treatment is that punishment expresses condemnation or disapproval of the conduct punished.[23] The person punished is blamed for what he did, and this explains the peculiar unfairness of punishing the innocent who are of course blameless.

But now, if we accept the idea that punishment involves the breach of a standard of conduct, how is this different from Quinton's point that punishment is always for an offence? The element of truth in Quinton's position is that there must be some wrongdoing or some offence for there to be punishment. But this is not to say that the person punished must be the offender. An innocent person can be punished for an offence committed by someone else. This can happen not only when the legal authority makes a mistake and punishes the wrong person, but also when it deliberately frames an innocent person.

[22] H. L. A. Hart, *The Concept of Law* (Oxford, 1961), p. 39.
[23] For an excellent discussion of this feature of punishment, see Joel Feinberg, 'The Expressive Function of Punishment', in Hyman Gross and Andrew von Hirsch (eds.), *Sentencing* (New York & Oxford, 1981).

But suppose now that my arguments fail, and Quinton's analysis of the concept of punishment is correct. It certainly does not follow that it is wrong to imprison innocent people or even to execute them. What follows is merely that we cannot *describe* these acts as *punishing* the innocent. But the real issue is a moral issue as to whether we are justified in inflicting suffering on innocent persons. Admittedly this is not exactly the same issue as whether we should *punish* the innocent which raises the additional problem of whether we may unjustly blame the blameless, but none the less it is a serious moral issue. Quinton argues that 'the suffering associated with punishment *may* not be inflicted on them, firstly, as brutal and secondly, if it is represented as punishment, as involving a lie.'[24] The second objection does not hold if we do not represent the infliction of suffering on the innocent as a form of punishment. And the first objection is not one of which utilitarians can avail themselves if the brutal treatment of the innocent will in fact produce the best consequences. So the argument against the utilitarian can now be reformulated as follows: why should we confine ourselves to punishment in those cases where the infliction of suffering on the innocent will produce the best consequences?

The objection to the utilitarian position is clearly moral, and hence it cannot be evaded by appealing even to a correct definition of the notion of punishment. A proper regard for the way in which terms are used will enable us to describe correctly the moral problem which confronts us, but it cannot solve that problem for us.

2.4. *The Disutility of Punishing the Innocent*

The second utilitarian response to the charge that utilitarians are committed to punishing the innocent draws our attention to the less obvious bad consequences of punishing innocent persons, and argues that on balance the punishment of the innocent will always produce worse consequences than the failure to do so. For example, it is claimed that the fact that an innocent man has been punished will soon leak out, and when that happens, there will be a loss of confidence in the

---

[24] 'On Punishment', p. 59.

sheriff and widespread fear among the population that any one of them might be the next innocent victim of the sheriff's attempt to prevent similar violence in future. Furthermore, the sheriff himself will have his sensibilities blunted once the barrier against framing and punishing the innocent has been removed. He is more likely to adopt a similar policy the next time he faces a problem of maintaining order, and on that occasion, there may be no strong utilitarian case for punishing an innocent person. It is also not certain that there will in fact be racial violence if an innocent person is not punished. On the other hand, the suffering of the innocent person who is punished is very real. The suffering of the innocent man is likely to be greater than that of the guilty. The punishment will come as a big shock to the innocent man, and he will be angered and distressed in a way that the guilty person will not be.[25]

But at each point of this utilitarian response, the critic can counter by tightening up the description of the example under consideration. Thus the sheriff suffers from a sudden fatal illness soon after the punishment of the innocent man, and he makes no death-bed confessions. No one else knows about the fabrication of evidence and the secret is buried with the sheriff. The innocent man who is punished has no relatives or close friends, and he himself is well endowed with an unusual temperament which faces unexpected disaster with calm resignation. We must not forget the unconvicted real offender who is still free and conceivably could give the whole show away. So he dies unexpectedly when he is run over by a bus on his way to the sheriff's funeral. Now we are back where we started with an example in which the punishment of an innocent person produces the best consequences and so should be accepted by the utilitarian.

2.5. *Fantastic Examples and Moral Principles*

But at this stage of the debate, the utilitarian will introduce a new, and by far the most complex and exciting, argument. He or she will argue that the nearer the critic gets to producing

---

[25] Some of these utilitarian objections to punishing the innocent are voiced by T. L. S. Sprigge, 'A Utilitarian Reply to Dr McCloskey', in Michael D. Bayles (ed.), *Contemporary Utilitarianism* (New York, 1968), pp. 278–82.

a water-tight example in which it is certain that punishing an innocent person will be optimific, the more fantastic the example becomes. The utilitarian moral theory cannot be defeated by the production of fantastic examples which are irrelevant to everyday moral argument in the real world.

It is strange that the rejection of fantastic examples has come to play such an important part in the writings of some utilitarian writers. In a radio talk 'Does Oxford Moral Philosophy Corrupt Youth?', Anscombe attacked the use of such examples by utilitarian-minded philosophers. She parodied their method of argument with an example in which you have to decide what you ought to do when you have to move forward but 'stepping with your right foot means killing twenty-five fine young men while stepping with your left foot would kill fifty drooling old ones'.[26] Rising to the occasion, Anscombe gives the answer: 'Obviously the right thing to do would be to jump and polish off the lot.'[27] Today the attacks on the use of fantastic examples in moral argument are much more likely to come from utilitarians, irritated by attempts to undermine their moral principles which proceed by way of showing that in some conceivable, but very unlikely, situations, they are committed to all sorts of monstrous and outrageous acts—the punishment and killing of innocent people, torture, racial and religious persecutions, etc.

I want to argue that there is an important role for fantastic examples in moral argument. I shall, for the time being at least, assume that it is only in fantastic situations that the punishment of the innocent will produce the best consequences.

Suppose that you make a moral judgement: 'It's wrong to stick knives into people.'[28] A philosopher replies: 'But suppose that human beings are so constructed that whenever you stick knives into their bodies you trigger off a mechanism which stimulates the pleasure-centres of their brains such that they

---

[26] G. E. M. Anscombe, 'Does Oxford Moral Philosophy Corrupt Youth?', *The Listener* (14 February 1957), p. 267.

[27] Ibid., p. 267.

[28] See the interesting discussion in Kai Nielsen, 'Against Moral Conservatism', in Karsten J. Struhl and Paula Rothenberg Struhl (eds.), *Ethics in Perspective* (New York, 1975), especially pp. 119–20. This article is reprinted from *Ethics*, 82 (1971–2), pp. 219–31.

experience very pleasurable sensations. Now surely it would then not be wrong to stick knives into them. Indeed mightn't it sometimes be obligatory to do so?' Is the philosopher just a smart Alec? Not necessarily. He or she may be trying to draw a distinction between, on the one hand, a subordinate or secondary moral principle, and on the other hand, a fundamental or ultimate moral principle. Sticking knives into people is only a subordinate moral principle: it is wrong only because it harms them. In the fantastic world imagined by the philosopher it would therefore not be wrong to stick knives into people. On the other hand the principle that we should not harm people may be a fundamental moral principle, and if it is, then, unlike a subordinate moral principle, it still holds good even in the fantastic world. In that world, it would not be wrong to stick knives into people, but it would still be wrong to harm them. Suppose that in the fantastic world, shaking hands would cause enormous pain. We would then have a new subordinate principle, applicable to that world, but not to our real world, that one ought not to shake hands unless both parties were masochists.

A subordinate moral principle is one which has to be justified in terms of another moral principle, whereas a fundamental moral principle is not justified by appealing to another moral principle. For the utilitarian, there is only one fundamental moral principle and that is the principle that one should always produce the best consequences. Thus from the utilitarian point of view the wrongness of punishing innocent people is only subordinate. It derives its justification from the fundamental utilitarian principle. It is wrong to punish the innocent only in so far as such punishment produces worse consequences than an alternative course of action. But for some non-utilitarians punishing the innocent is itself a fundamental moral principle. Our discussion of the philosopher's example suggests that fundamental moral principles apply even to fantastic situations. If this is correct, then we have a good reason for using fantastic examples to test the fundamental utilitarian principle. Utilitarians cannot therefore claim that their principle is only applicable to the real world and thereby refuse to consider the implications of the principle in fantastic situations. They can only fall back on this argument if the principle is subordinate, but it is not.

Furthermore, since subordinate principles do not apply to all situations whereas fundamental principles do, we can use fantastic situations to help us decide whether a particular principle is subordinate or fundamental. The principle that we are presently interested in is about the wrongness of punishing the innocent. We want to decide whether this principle is derivable from the utilitarian principle. If it is, then it is a subordinate principle. But if it is wrong to punish the innocent even when such punishment will produce the best consequences, then the utilitarian principle cannot be the only fundamental moral principle. We will not have shown that the wrongness of punishing the innocent is itself fundamental, for it may be based on a non-utilitarian fundamental moral principle. But even showing that much is enough to refute the utilitarian theory of punishment as providing the only basis for the justification of punishment.

In an interesting defence of consequentialism against moral absolutism, Kai Nielsen argues: 'What is brutal or vile, for example, throwing a knife at a human being just for the fun of it, would not be so, if human beings were invulnerable to harm from such a direction because they had a metallic exo-skeleton. Similarly, what is, as things are, morally intolerable, for example, the judicial killing of the innocent, need not be morally intolerable in all conceivable circumstances.'[29] The two cases are however different in that the wrongness of throwing a knife at a human being just for the fun of it is clearly subordinate to some fundamental principle like that of not harming innocent human beings. On the other hand, for some non-utilitarians, the injunction against the judicial killing of the innocent is not a subordinate principle but an instance of a fundamental non-utilitarian moral principle against the killing of the innocent. Even if Nielsen is right that such a non-utilitarian principle may be violated in some conceivable circumstances, this does not show that the principle derives its force from consequentialist considerations. A non-utilitarian fundamental moral principle need not be absolutist in the sense that it must never be violated no matter what the

[29] Ibid., p. 120.

consequences. It may sometimes be overridden by utilitarian considerations. But even when it is overridden, it 'applies' or 'holds good' in the sense that it embodies a morally relevant consideration which has to be taken into account in deciding what to do. (It has 'the dimension of weight' that Ronald Dworkin attributes to legal principles as opposed to legal rules, so that even when a legal principle does not determine or necessitate a particular decision, it still states a reason that argues in one direction rather than another.)[30]

Thus some moderate non-utilitarians will side with utilitarian against the absolutist when for example the failure to punish or to harm an innocent person produces very much worse consequences to others than the harm caused to the innocent. In such a case although moderate non-utilitarians give a negative moral weight to punishing or harming the innocent, which is independent of utilitarian considerations, the weight may not be good enough to outweigh the positive weight which both they and the utilitarian give to avoidance of a great deal of suffering to others. But sometimes the consequences of punishing or harming the innocent can be *clearly better* than the consequences of not punishing or harming even though they are not *much better*, and in such situations whereas the utilitarian would still punish or harm the innocent, the moderate non-utilitarian would not. This difference has not been sufficiently appreciated because of the ambiguity in the claim that the consequences of one act are clearly better than those of all alternative acts. Sometimes what we mean is that the consequences are much better. But sometimes the difference is clearly better when it is only slightly better, but it is clear that it is slightly better. The clarity here refers not to the size of the difference but to the vividness of our perception of the difference. Thus under appropriate conditions, a person who is 5′8″ tall can be clearly taller than a person who is 5′7″ because, although the difference in height is small, it is clear that there is a small difference. The relevance of this to our discussion is that in situations where the consequences of punishing or harming the innocent, relative to all other alternative courses of action, are clearly, even though only slightly,

better in this sense, the utilitarian would regard such punishment or harm as justifiably inflicted. But now moderate non-
utilitarians would disagree because the independent negative
weight they give to punishing or harming the innocent is
enough to override the slightly better consequences.

If, as we are now assuming to be true, there are no actual
situations in which the punishment of the innocent will produce
the best consequences, then we have a good reason for
appealing to fantastic situations. In the real world both the
utilitarian and the non-utilitarian will, for different reasons,
believe it wrong to punish the innocent. We need therefore a
fantastic situation in which the utilitarian and non-utilitarian
responses will diverge to discover which is more plausible. In
this context the role played by fantastic examples is rather
like that of controlled experiments in science. Suppose that
when two factors, A and B, are present together we get an
effect E. But suppose further that in the natural world A and
B are inseparable. Scientists may wish to find out whether it
is A or B singly, or the combination of them, which causes
the effect E. To do this they will artificially create in the
laboratory situations in which A and B are isolated from each
other and then see whether E will still be produced. To object
to the scientists' work on the ground that in the natural world
A and B are inseparable is to show a considerable misun-
derstanding of what is going on. Of course the analogy is
appropriate only up to a point. The fantastic example is supposed to separate what in the real world is inseparable, namely,
the very bad consequences of punishing the innocent and the
injustice of such punishment. But the fantastic example cannot
provide a conclusive argument against the utilitarian principle
because it is always open to the utilitarian to reject the view
that punishing the innocent is still wrong when it produces
the best consequences, in the way that it is not open for someone to claim that A alone causes E when it is shown that B
singly can also cause E. But confronting utilitarians with a
situation that they will not face in the real world helps them,
and others who may be attracted by their view, to appreciate
more clearly its implications. It is one thing to know in the
abstract that we are committed to all sorts of actions which
promote the best consequences. But it is quite another thing

to know in vivid detail some of the numerous implications that
our principle has in various circumstances. Well chosen fantastic examples will help us to understand the nature of our
fundamental moral principles and their underlying assumptions.

But I have said enough to explain why I think that there
is a place for fantastic examples in moral argument. I cannot
therefore accept the vigorous attack on fantastic examples put
forward by Sprigge, who argues: 'A utilitarian will see no point
in trying to imagine oneself looking with approval on the imagi-
nary situation, since this is likely to weaken the feelings while
not serving as a preparation for any actual situation.'[31] His
point is that if in the real world the punishment of the innocent
will never produce the best consequences, then the utilitarian
will develop strong feelings of aversion towards such punishment. They cause unnecessary harm. But if we now confront
the utilitarian with a fantastic situation in which the punishment of the innocent is justified on utilitarian grounds, then
the utilitarian will acknowledge this fact. But he will be uneasy
because he has an aversion towards punishing the innocent
which was built up through his experience in the real world.
He does not wish to dwell on fantastic examples because they
will weaken his strong feelings against punishing the innocent.
He has every reason to sustain these feelings since he is not
ever going to be confronted with a situation in the real world
in which he would endorse the punishment of the innocent.

But Sprigge's argument seems to miss the point about the
use of fantastic example. He *assumes* that the utilitarian principle is the correct fundamental principle and uses it to decide
what disposition he should cultivate. If one takes for granted
that utilitarianism is correct, then one would have utilitarian
reasons for doing or abstaining from many actions. For example one might decide not even to argue with non-utilitarians
for fear that this might weaken one's utilitarian dispositions.
But the issue with which we are concerned is whether
utilitarianism is a correct moral doctrine. Fantastic examples
will help us decide by illuminating the assumptions and implications of utilitarianism and of alternative principles. Even

---

[31] T. L. S. Sprigge, 'A Utilitarian Reply to Dr McCloskey', p. 275.

though a fantastic situation will never occur in the real world, it can, by presenting us with relatively simple and sharp alternatives, help us to understand the nature and strength of our commitment to various values. Even a person already inclined towards utilitarianism cannot afford to allow dispositions based on the acceptance of subordinate moral principles to develop into prejudices with a life of their own, and cut off from the fundamental utilitarian principle which is for him their ultimate justification. As situations in the world change, new subordinate moral principles are necessary to replace old ones or to supplement them. But fundamental principles do not change and hence it is important that we decide the status of various principles.

But Sprigge has another argument against the use of fantastic examples. He points out that we may not be able to focus properly on a fantastic example. Certain features of the real world are absent in the fantastic example, but because we are used to these features, we may unwittingly smuggle them into the fantastic example. Thus in the real world punishing an innocent person will produce very bad consequences. However, in a fantastic example, such bad consequences are explicitly ruled out and it is, on the other hand, stipulated that there will be some very good consequences. But Sprigge points out, 'If one finds oneself still half-inclined to call such punishment wrong, it may well be because one does not really succeed in envisaging the situation just as described, but surrounds it with those circumstances of real life which would in fact create a greater probability of unhappiness in its consequences than happiness.'[32]

There is certainly some truth in Sprigge's comments and we can bring this out more clearly by considering the details of a type of fantastic example which is sometimes used against the hedonistic utilitarian. The hedonistic utilitarian believes that pleasure is the only thing intrinsically good, or good in itself, and pain is the only thing intrinsically bad, and that we should always act to maximize the total amount of pleasure. Imagine a world in which there are nurses and doctors who are dedicated to their patients, but who secretly get a peculiar

[32] Ibid., p. 276.

form of sadistic pleasure out of the patients' suffering. This sadism is peculiar because it does not affect the conduct of the nurses and doctors towards their patients. They never allow their patients to suffer one moment longer than is necessary. Nor do they display their enjoyment of their patients' suffering in any way that will distress others. So perhaps we are to imagine them having their tea-breaks in some remote corner of the hospital and rejoicing at their patients' suffering, but then returning with renewed vigour to attend to the patients. If the hedonistic utilitarian had a choice between creating two worlds, one in which there are these doctors and nurses, and another in which everything else is exactly the same except that the doctors and nurses are not sadistic, then he or she would create the first world. But the critic points out that this is surely wrong in spite of the fact that there will be more pleasure in the first world. If we agree with the critic, can we be sure that our preference for the second world is not based on our failure to envisage the first world exactly as it has been presented to us? Perhaps we tend to smuggle into the first world the wide-ranging effects that sadism normally has. We might therefore find it difficult to come to terms with the innocent sadism of the doctors and nurses. Perhaps we do not fully appreciate that their innocent sadism is good only for a few harmless laughs, and there is no danger of the doctors and nurses prolonging the suffering of their patients when no one else is around. And if we clearly confront the fantastic example as it is described then perhaps we may well agree with the hedonistic utilitarian that we ought to create the first world in preference to the second. Sprigge's argument does appear to be quite powerful when applied to this kind of fantastic example. But it is not an argument which shows that fantastic examples as such have no place in moral reasoning. What the argument does is to warn us of the dangers of not considering fantastic examples as they are described, and of using fantastic examples which involve too radical a change in human nature or in the world in which we live. Thus although it is logically possible for there to be 'innocent sadists', it is difficult to imagine why they will not prolong the suffering of their patients if they gain so much pleasure from the suffering. But this difficulty may in the end be purely subjective, and the example may still be usefully employed in arguing with some people. In any case, examples can be fantastic in the sense of being very unlikely to occur in the real world even though they do not involve radical distortions of human nature or the world in which we live. An unusual combination of individually familiar circumstances may be most unlikely, but there is normally no difficulty in imagining its occurrence. Cases in real life may involve too complex assessments of the consequences of our actions, and those with different views will be bogged down in purely factual disagreements. So there is sometimes an advantage in using a fantastic example in which we can stipulate the consequences of certain actions so that discussion can then focus on the fundamental moral issues at stake.

Another attack on the use of fantastic examples is made by R. M. Hare in his stimulating defence of utilitarianism particularly in his book *Moral Thinking: Its Levels, Method and Point.*[33] Hare makes an important and illuminating distinction between two levels of moral thinking—the intuitive level and the critical level. We need relatively simple moral principles to help us decide what to do in everyday life when we are faced with new situations which resemble past situations in some important respects. Without such principles we will have to face each new situation from scratch and decide what to do without the benefit of useful dispositions developed through the adoption and application of such principles. These principles will also protect us from the temptation to special pleading which leads us to think in a manner which suits our own interests at the expense of the interests of others. Thus if we do not adopt the principle that lying is wrong, we are likely to persuade ourselves that in a particular situation the benefit of a lie to us is enormous and the harm to others only slight when in fact, if we view the situation impartially, we will discover that the lie causes much greater harm than good. So far we are operating at the intuitive level where our thinking is constrained by limitations of time and knowledge. But moral thinking cannot end at this level for there may be conflicts in the moral principles which we adopt at the intuitive level and

[33] R. M. Hare, *Moral Thinking: Its Levels, Method and Point* (Oxford, 1981), esp. Chs. 1–3 and 8–9.

these have to be resolved at another level, the critical level, where we are not subject to the limitations present at the intuitive level. Critical thinking is also necessary to determine whether a principle at the intuitive level is applicable to a new situation which differs from the cases covered by the principle in some important respects, and more generally to decide on the right course of action in unusual situations. Hare thinks that at the critical level the principle to be adopted is one which calls for the maximization of the satisfaction of preferences or desires, and this is a version of utilitarianism that is sometimes called preference utilitarianism. I shall not be concerned here with his argument for utilitarianism. But in the light of his distinction between the two levels of moral thinking, Hare would relegate the principle that it is wrong to punish the innocent to the intuitive level.[34]

Principles at the intuitive level are selected by critical thinking. We select those principles whose acceptance will produce actions which will best approximate to those actions which an archangel with superhuman qualities and no human weaknesses will recommend when he engages in critical thinking. For Hare, this means that the principles to be accepted at the intuitive level are those which will best promote the utilitarian end of maximizing the satisfaction of desires in the actual world.

Hare points out that the opponents of utilitarianism use fantastic examples in order to show that in such cases the utilitarian answers as to how we should act conflict with our common intuitions grounded on the acceptance of principles at the intuitive level.[35] But such conflicts do not undermine utilitarianism because our common intuitions about, for example, the wrongness of punishing the innocent, are designed for the actual world, and might not be appropriate to fantastic situations which do not occur in the actual world. So if, in fantastic situations, utilitarianism recommends the punishment of the innocent, then this does not show that utilitarianism is in any way defective. Hare challenges the critic of utilitarianism to specify the level at which his fantastic

[34] Ibid. pp. 162–3. Hare's argument for utilitarianism is critically discussed by Bernard Williams, *Ethics and the Limits of Philosophy* (London, 1985), pp. 82–92.
[35] Ibid., pp. 48–9.

examples are to be considered. If they are brought in at the intuitive level then they are irrelevant since they do not refer to situations which will occur in the actual world. Hare maintains that fantastic examples are admissible at the critical level, but argues that at this level no appeal can be made to moral intuitions which cannot cope with such unusual cases.[36]

Hare's insistence that the discussion should be conducted *either* at the intuitive level *or* at the critical level is a little unfair. This is because a principle about the wrongness of punishing innocent people is simple enough to be used at the intuitive level, but at the same time it might also embody moral considerations which have an irreducible role to play at the critical level. At the critical level, it might well be, as we shall see later, that the intuitive principle, couched in exceptionless terms, would need to be qualified. But this does not mean that the moral consideration embodied in the principle is only derivative from other considerations and does not itself make an independent moral claim on us. As a utilitarian, Hare has a critical principle which specifies only one type of moral consideration as relevant, the maximization of the satisfaction of desires. This is the utilitarian end, and the intuitive principles are selected on the basis of their relative superiority in promoting this end in the actual world. These intuitive principles can be specified independently of the utilitarian end. The formulations of the principles do not *require* any reference to the maximization of desires. The relation between them and utilitarianism is simply that of means to end. The intuitive principles therefore cannot be chosen on the basis of the critical principle alone, but must be sensitive to the social situations in the actual world in which intuitive principles are to be applied. It is likely that in different societies different intuitive principles will be selected. But those non-utilitarians who believe that certain actions are intrinsically right or wrong, and that punishing the innocent is one such type of intrinsically wrong act, will view the relation between critical and intuitive principles differently. At least some of their intuitive principles will be relatively constant across cultural and social differences, and they will represent a more generalized version of their

---

[36] Ibid., pp. 131–2.

critical principles. They are not means to the realization of
the non-utilitarian critical principles but rather imperfect
exemplifications of those principles. They are imperfect
because at the critical level the intuitive principles would have
to be qualified since there are situations in which two such
principles may conflict. Thus at the critical level we might
discover that we are prepared to override the unqualified
wrongness of punishing the innocent if large enough harms
are avoided by such punishment. But this does not mean that
the wrongness of punishing the innocent is simply dependent
on the badness of the consequences it produces. Both the
utilitarian and the non-utilitarian might agree at the intuitive
level without also agreeing at the critical level. Hare allows
the appeal to fantastic examples at the critical level, and such
appeals may be necessary to clarify the nature of the principles
that we are prepared to accept at that level. Thus a fundamental issue to be settled at that level is whether critical moral
thinking is controlled by one principle, as Hare and other
utilitarians suggest, or whether it has to find room for an
irreducible plurality of moral principles as many non-utilitarians believe.[37]

But now once the discussion shifts to the critical level, are
we not caught in the grips of Hare's argument that even though
fantastic examples are permissible, the appeal to moral intuitions is not? So the fact that utilitarianism conflicts with our
moral intuitions cannot be used as an argument against
utilitarianism. Hare sometimes refers disparagingly to these
anti-utilitarian moral intuitions as 'the received opinion' and
argues that they have no probative force.[38] Thus he points out
that as recently as the early twentieth century the received
opinion was against 'mixed bathing' even though 'mixed
bathing' had a utilitarian justification.[39] The example is well
chosen for at a time when nude bathing is the issue, and when
some energy-conscious bodies are urging us to have 'mixed
showers', it is unlikely that anyone today would share the

[37] See Stuart Hampshire, *Two Theories of Morality* (Oxford 1977).
[38] *Moral Thinking: Its Levels, Method and Point*, op. cit., p. 12. See also 'The Argument
from Received Opinion', in R. M. Hare, *Essays on Philosophical Method* (London 1971),
p. 122.
[39] 'The Argument from Received Opinion' p. 127.

previously received opinion that there was something wrong with men and women, amply clothed, enjoying the same beaches together. The example shows that received opinion can embody prejudices, and therefore moral intuitions of this kind should not be used at the critical level. Indeed, Hare argues that moral intuitions should be modified by critical thinking which will inculcate the *right* intuitions whether or not these coincide with the received opinions.[40]

Hare's argument is successful against those who use moral intuitions as bed-rock considerations round which critical thinking must be constructed. But that is not the way that fantastic examples have featured in our discussion so far. I have pointed out that we appeal to fantastic examples to better appreciate the implications of our fundamental moral commitments. If we cannot accept some of these implications then we have to give up or modify our fundamental moral values. Thus utilitarians would have to accept all the implications of utilitarianism in actual and hypothetical situations, and if they want us to accept utilitarianism, then they must also persuade us that none of these implications is unacceptable to us. Fantastic examples have an honourable role to play even within the framework of Hare's moral theory. For in his theory to accept a moral judgement is to accept a universal prescription, and to accept a prescription is to act on it. The utilitarian principle that one ought always to produce the best consequences is itself a generalized moral judgement which identifies only one feature of actions as being relevant, namely the consequences produced. This being the case, anyone who accepts that principle must be prepared to act in all situations, actual or fantastic, in which the action will produce the best consequences. Fantastic examples help to test the genuineness and the strength of a person's commitment to utilitarianism. It is inadequate for a utilitarian to respond, in advance of a consideration of specific examples, that he or she is prepared to accept all the implications of utilitarianism. The utilitarian can of course be sure that whenever utilitarianism is inconsistent with a particular moral judgement others are inclined to

---

[40] *Moral Thinking: Its Levels, Method and Point*, p. 142. A different view of the relation between intuitions and general moral principles or ethical theories is given by Bernard Williams, *Ethics and the Limits of Philosophy*, Ch. 6.

accept, then that particular moral judgement will involve the acceptance of a course of action which will not produce the best consequences. But it is one thing to know this in general terms; it is quite another thing to repudiate all such particular judgements in the vast variety of situations in which they involve the non-production of the best consequences. Utilitarians may well find that in a particular case their insufficiently tested faith in their ability to resist recalcitrant counter-examples is in fact misplaced. Their moral beliefs may be more complex than they suppose, and utilitarianism may not be able to impose an order on their thinking.[41] What is true of the professed utilitarian will also be true of any person engaged in moral thinking. Fantastic examples probe the depths of our thinking. In using such examples, we are not appealing to the received opinion, but to the reflective judgement of each party to a moral argument as to how he or she would respond to particular situations. No matter how moral agents arrive at their critical moral principles, they still have to be sure that they know and can accept the implications of these principles.

2.6. *Moral Dilemmas and Complexities*

I have so far only been concerned to explain and justify the use of fantastic examples in moral argument. But we cannot assume that once fantastic examples are introduced, utilitarianism rather than non-utilitarian moral beliefs will be in difficulties. The conclusion that it is sometimes right to punish the innocent is one to which utilitarians are committed, but this may well be the correct conclusion. Certainly some non-utilitarians will share this conclusion. I have already mentioned this possibility earlier in our discussion. There are different ways of reaching the same moral conclusion in a particular case, and I shall now argue that even if the utilitarian's answer in a particular case, fantastic or otherwise, is correct, his or her reasoning to that answer may not be as illuminating as a non-utilitarian approach.

Let us consider a different example in which some non-utilitarians will also agree with the utilitarian that the normally strong moral injunction against torturing human beings may have to be violated. Anthony Quinton gives the example of 'a

---

[41] See Stuart Hampshire, *Two Theories of Morality*, pp. 26–7.

man planting a bomb in a large hospital, which no one but
he knows how to defuse and no one dare touch for fear of
setting it off'.[42] Quinton thinks that torturing the man could
be justifiable given that it is an emergency situation with no
time to resort to other methods, and there is no doubt about
the bomb-planter's responsibility for, or capacity to produce,
the violent act. The bomb-planter's responsibility for the act,
and the fact that a much greater degree of suffering will be
experienced by the innocent patients and staff of the hospital
if the bomb were not defused in time, are certainly morally
relevant features of the situation. But it is unclear whether
these features can best be accounted for within the utilitarian
framework of thinking. The example suggests that utilitarianism can mount a powerful attack on at least some forms of
moral absolutism which share the view that there are certain
kinds of acts, of which torture is one, which are always wrong,
irrespective of the consequences.

But suppose now that the bomb-planter shows a considerable capacity for withstanding or evading torture (perhaps he
conveniently faints whenever he is about to be tortured). There
is very little time left, but it is discovered that the bomb-planter
has a wife to whom he is very attached. If a moderate amount
of physical pain were inflicted on her, the bomb-planter will
defuse the bomb. Would it be wrong to harm his wife? This
is in some ways like a case in which the punishment of an
innocent person will prevent very bad consequences from
occurring. If the pain to be inflicted on the innocent wife is
very much less than the suffering of the people in the hospital,
then both utilitarians and some non-utilitarians will agree that
the act is justifiable. But does it follow that, other things being
equal, we would be prepared to inflict the same amount of
physical suffering on the wife as we would on the bomb-planter
himself? Suppose we had a choice between torturing the bomb-
planter and inflicting slightly less suffering on his innocent
wife to achieve the same result. The fact that he is responsible
for planting the bomb whereas she is innocent should be
sufficient for us to choose him rather than her. This shows
that we attach some weight, independent of utilitarian considerations, to not using innocent people unjustly for the benefit

[42] Anthony M. Quinton, 'Views', *The Listener* (2 December 1971), p. 758.

of others. On the other hand, there is no similar injustice in making the bomb-planter suffer if it is through his own act that we are confronted with the situation in which his suffering is the lesser of two evils. We would of course regret that we had to choose between two evils, and some might also regard torture as an evil requiring a special justification. Utilitarianism cannot adequately capture the injustice of using innocent people as means towards desirable ends because it treats the difference between torturing the bomb-planter and torturing his innocent wife as merely a difference in the consequences of the respective acts.

Let us pursue further the claim that utilitarianism does not do justice to the complexity of moral thinking. Suppose now that our notorious bomb-planter has placed a peculiar bomb in a large children's hospital such that if the bomb exploded it will release a gas which will cause all those in the hospital to experience an unpleasant itch for just a couple of minutes. But the side effects are that all future direct descendants of the inhabitants of the hospital will also, once in a lifetime, each experience a two-minute unpleasant itch. There is no possibility of a cure, but there are no bad consequences. In a few generations, the total undesirable consequences of the bomb's explosion is that thousands of people will have each experienced such two-minute itches. Let us assume that the only way to prevent the explosion of the bomb is to torture the innocent child of the bomb-planter. In such a situation it would be wrong to torture the innocent child no matter how many other people would each suffer two-minute itches if we did not torture. But this is precisely the conclusion that the utilitarian cannot accept because although each person suffers only a little, if there are many such sufferers, the bad consequences when added together, will sooner or later exceed the great suffering of the tortured child. As the well-known rhymes go:

> Little drops of water,
>   Little grains of sand,
> Make the mighty ocean
>   And the pleasant land.

So too, little two-minute itches can add up to one mighty pain.

If pleasures and pains can be aggregated, as utilitarians believe, then the lesser pains of many people can exceed the much greater pain of one person. No matter how great the suffering of being tortured, it is still a finite amount that can be exceeded. No matter how slight the unpleasantness of an itch may be, if there are enough people experiencing it, then the aggregate will exceed the agony of one person being tortured. The only way in which utilitarians can get round this is by introducing certain discontinuities of scale in which, for example, no aggregate of the much lesser pains of many persons can outweigh the great suffering caused by the torture of one person. But this would be an *ad hoc* device which can find no motivation within utilitarianism itself, and will destroy some of its distinctive features. It is irrelevant from the utilitarian point of view that in the case of the tortured child all the great suffering is experienced by one person, whereas in the case of the little itches the unpleasantness is spread out very thinly over many people, and no single person experiences the total suffering.[43] Utilitarians are only interested in the distribution of good and bad consequences when this affects the total. An equal distribution of benefits and burdens is not in itself better than a very unequal one if the two distributions yield the same total happiness or welfare. In the actual world, differences in distribution will of course often affect the total welfare, but the fantastic example helps to bring out the point that in certain situations utilitarians are committed to sacrificing the major interest of one person in order to promote the minor interests of many persons. In practice this commitment would lead to the justification of the exemplary punishment of an offender for a relatively trivial offence if this would deter many others from committing similar offences. This is an issue to which we will return.

Let me summarize my objections to the utilitarian theory because these objections have to be taken into account in constructing a more acceptable theory of punishment. The first objection is that the utilitarian theory does not give any independent weight to the injustice of punishing the innocent.

[43] Some critics have accused utilitarianism of ignoring 'the separateness of persons'. For an illuminating discussion, see H. L. A. Hart, 'Between Utility and Rights', in H. L. A. Hart, *Essays in Jurisprudence and Philosophy* (Oxford, 1983).

If the theory regards such punishment as wrong, then it is wrong simply in virtue of the fact that it produces bad consequences. Secondly, there are situations in which the utilitarian theory permits and even requires us to inflict great suffering on one person in order to prevent many other persons from each experiencing a very much smaller amount of suffering.

2.7. A Return to the Real World

I have so far assumed, for the sake of argument, that it is only in fantastic situations that utilitarians are committed to punishing the innocent. But it is now time to say something about this assumption. Most utilitarians seem to make the assumption. Thus Hare writes: 'The retributivists are right at the intuitive level, and the utilitarians at the critical level.'[44] But contrast this with David Richards's claim in *The Moral Criticism of Law* that the utilitarian theory of punishment 'clearly seems to allow and even require the punishment of the innocent, since it is very plausible that a higher degree of criminal deterrence would be achieved by punishing the children or relatives or friends or lovers of criminals in addition to or even in place of the criminal. Primitive systems of law often do exactly this, . . .'[45] In the face of these conflicting claims, two remarks are appropriate. First, no one can claim with confidence that, on the balance of probabilities, there are no actual cases in which punishing the innocent will produce the best consequences. But secondly, the strength of our conviction, which is shared by many utilitarians, that punishing the innocent in the real world is unjustified, cannot be accounted for simply on the basis of utilitarian considerations. If we were guided by purely utilitarian considerations, we would not be entitled to be as confident as we in fact are that such punishment in the real world is wrong, and we should indeed be prepared to experiment with limited proposals for the punishment of the innocent.

Indeed we can go further and argue that in the present state of our knowledge, surveyed earlier, the evidence of the desirable effects of punishment is not always as firmly based as is

[44] *Moral Thinking: Its Levels, Method and Point*, p. 163.
[45] David A. J. Richards, *The Moral Criticism of Law* (Encino & Belmont, 1977), pp. 232–3.

often assumed, and this presents some difficulties for a purely utilitarian justification of punishment. From the utilitarian point of view punishing offenders produces bad consequences which are certain and not speculative, namely the suffering inflicted directly by punishment on offenders and indirectly on their friends and relatives. Against this, there is no equally firm evidence, in all cases where punishment is thought to be justified, of its countervailing good effects. There is some evidence of incapacitative effects although the extent of these effects varies with different types of offences, and the evidence is also consistent with there being some general deterrent effect. Again, there is good reason to think that the total abandonment of the practice of punishment would have unfortunate results. But there are specific crimes in which the utilitarian case for punishment, while not ruled out, is not particularly strong. It is then unclear what we should do in the present state of our knowledge if we were guided by purely utilitarian considerations. In fact our thinking on these matters is also guided by non-utilitarian considerations. Other things being equal, we think it better that the guilty should suffer through punishment than that there should be similar suffering by the innocent victims of crime. Again, given that the practice of punishment has some utilitarian justification, there will also be offenders who may justifiably be punished by appealing to non-utilitarian considerations. For example, if the punishment for some offences can be justified on utilitarian grounds in terms of the general deterrent effect and the incapacitative effect of such punishment, then it is unfair to allow those who have committed more serious offences to go unpunished even if in these latter cases the existing evidence is inadequate to show that punishment has similar good effects.

I do not believe that the practice of punishment would be justified if there were a decisive utilitarian case against it, or if it did not at least have some utilitarian support. But this is not to say that all desirable aspects of that practice can be justified in purely utilitarian terms.

3

RETRIBUTIVE THEORIES

3.1. *Introduction*

THERE is no complete agreement about what sorts of theories are retributive except that all such theories try to establish an essential link between punishment and moral wrongdoing. But so-called retributive theories vary in scope, in the type of reasons they offer for punishment, in the strength of these reasons, and in their accounts of how punishment should fit the crime.

In this chapter I shall focus on the different retributive reasons for punishment. Although I give retributive theories a fairly sympathetic hearing, I shall conclude that they are all flawed in one way or another. Even the most plausible of them underdetermines the case for punishment and requires support from non-retributive considerations.

3.2. *Punishment Annuls Crime*

One historically important version of the retributive theory is embodied in the Hegelian claim that punishment 'annuls' the crime. This claim has been dismissed by critics on the ground that no act of punishment which is inflicted after the crime has already been committed can annul it. The past cannot be changed: the murder, for example, has taken place, and even if the murderer is executed, the result is two deaths as against no deaths before the crime was committed. It is claimed by these critics that punishment cannot restore the situation to what it was, and it cannot therefore cancel out the crime.

However, in some cases the victims of crime can be compensated for the harm done to them. But even if the compensation is such that a victim is indifferent between two situations, one in which the crime never took place, and the other in which a criminal act was committed followed by an 'equivalent' amount of compensation, it is clear that compensation is not the same as punishment. The focus of compensation is on repairing the harm done to victims, and not on depriving the offender of something he values. It is of course true that in particular cases, victims may be compensated at the expense of offenders. But this is not essential to the notion of compensation. Indeed many of those who are concerned about compensating victims of crime see a role for the State in providing the resources for compensation. This is often necessary in the case of financial compensation. For where such compensation is substantial, it would be impossible to extract all of it from offenders, even if a scheme could be devised whereby offenders, as part of their punishment, were required to work and give their earnings to their victims.

So the view that punishment annuls crime has been regarded as incoherent, or at best a doctrine of compensation. These objections hit their target if the notion that punishment annuls crime is interpreted in any sense which implies that when an offence is annulled the harm that is caused is somehow wiped out, and the world is restored to its original state before the crime was committed. But recently David E. Cooper has given a detailed and very ingenious interpretation of Hegel which suggests a different, and more plausible, account of the notion of 'annulment'.[1]

Cooper compares the notion of annulment here with that of an annulment of a verdict of Guilty. It is an historical fact that at his trial the defendant was found guilty, and that fact cannot be changed. But by going through a certain procedure we establish that the past verdict was a mistake. The defendant was never really guilty, and it is in that sense that the verdict is annulled. Similarly, Cooper claims that Hegel's view is that the victim of crime has certain rights which the criminal is implicitly denying. Although the criminal does not necessarily intend to deny the rights of his victim, the failure to punish the criminal is tantamount to an admission that an explicit denial of rights would have been correct. Punishment annuls crime in the sense that it establishes that the victim has those rights, and hence the criminal's denial of them is a mistake. Punishment is said by Hegel 'to restore the right',

[1] David E. Cooper, 'Hegel's Theory of Punishment', in Z. A. Pelcynski (ed.), *Hegel's Political Philosophy: Problems and Perspectives* (Cambridge, 1971). Cooper discusses Hegel's *Philosophy of Right*, translated by T. M. Knox (Oxford, 1942).

and Cooper interprets this to mean that punishment establishes with certainty that the right exists.

Cooper's reconstruction of Hegel's doctrine is dependent
on the view that legal rights are what Cooper calls 'performatees'. Performatees owe their existence to certain
rule-governed performances. Thus promises are performatees
in that if a person is to make a promise, he or she must go
through some rule-governed procedure like saying, under
appropriate conditions, 'I promise . . .'. The existence of legal
rights depends on some rule or convention like a written statute
or a judicial decision. But while the existence of the relevant
rule is a necessary condition for the existence of a legal right,
it is not a sufficient condition because the rule may not be
enforced. This brings Cooper to the central cases in which a
legal right is said to exist. He maintains that 'attempting to
apprehend and punish men is a form of procedure necessary
to establish that rights of a certain kind exist in any paradig-
matic manner.'[2]

Cooper's account ties the justification of punishment to the
justification of the relevant legal rights. For if ascribing certain
rights to people is justified, and if further the existence of
these rights implies that those who have violated the rights
are to be punished, then it follows that punishment is justified.
Without punishment there could not logically be legal rights,
in the same way that without some form of ceremony, like the
exchange of rings, there could be no marriage. Punishment is
not a useful means to the preservation of rights, for this implies
that punishment and rights are distinct. Just as putting on
the ring is part of what constitutes the act of getting married,
so too the punishment of those who violate people's rights is
part of what it is for people to have rights.

Cooper himself explores a major objection to this view of
punishment. If we grant that legal rights are performatees in
the sense that when they are infringed, some public action
must be taken against violators, it still does not follow that
the action must be in the form of punishment. Why isn't the
public verbal denunciation of criminals sufficient to establish
the existence of legal rights? Cooper's reply is that such denunciation of crime would not be feared by the criminal, and

² Ibid., p. 162.

would not therefore be as effective as punishment in checking criminal behaviour. But this reply shows that punishment has to be justified in terms of its desirable consequences, and not just in terms of its alleged logical connection with the legal rights of victims of crime. On the account of legal rights as performatees, all that is needed for the existence of such rights is that legal officials take *some* action to show their disapproval of those who infringe the rights. But we could have a legal system in which judges are empowered to publicly denounce criminals to varying degrees of intensity depending on the relative importance of the rights that criminals have violated. For example, if the offender infringes a minor legal right, he receives a mild dressing down from a magistrate. But for the violation of major legal rights strong public denunciation will be delivered by the highest court of the land. In a legal system of this kind, it can be said that the public denunciation of criminals is a form of punishment. But the point is that we would not accept such punishments in our legal system if they were not effective in reducing crime. The notion of legal rights as performatees cannot explain why punishment should take the form of imprisonment and fines rather than a ritualized form of public verbal denunciation.

Similar objections can be raised against 'the denunciatory theory of punishment' which Lord Denning at one time proposed, and which is sometimes regarded as a version of the retributive theory. According to Denning, it is a mistake 'to consider the object of punishment as being deterrent or reformative or preventive and nothing else. . . The ultimate justification of any punishment is not that it is a deterrent, but that it is the emphatic denunciation by the community of a crime: and from this point of view there are some murders which, in the present state of public opinion, demand the most emphatic denunciation of all, namely the death penalty.'[3]

There are many objections to Denning's theory. For example, Hart argues that the law should not simply reflect uninstructed public opinion about the moral seriousness of various crimes but should help to shape popular sentiments.[4]

[3] Quoted by H. L. A. Hart, *Punishment and Responsibility* (Oxford, 1968), p. 170.
[4] Ibid., pp. 170–3. See also Nigel Walker, *Punishment, Danger and Stigma* (Oxford, 1980), pp. 28–30.

Again, Hart points out that the social morality that judges are supposed to reflect when they denounce criminals is not homogeneous for we live in a morally plural society. But the most fundamental objection is that Denning's theory does not explain why the denunciation of crime should take the form of imprisoning or even executing offenders rather than merely denouncing them verbally.[5] We can express our moral condemnation of criminal conduct without depriving criminals of their liberties or their lives. It is important, as Hart points out, to distinguish between Denning's denunciatory theory which seeks to provide a *justification* of punishment from the different view that it is one of the *defining features* of legal punishment that it expresses the community's condemnation of the offender's act.[6] It is quite consistent to adopt the latter view while believing that the punishment is unjustified and should not be inflicted, or that the justification of punishment is in terms of its deterrent, reformative, or incapacitative effects.

Both Cooper's interpretation of Hegel and Denning's denunciatory theory try to justify punishment in terms of its function in publicly condemning crime. This tradition is continued and developed by Robert Nozick.

3.3. *Nozick's Retributivism: Connecting with Correct Values*

In his recent book *Philosophical Explanations,* Nozick presents what is in many ways the most inventive, if somewhat obscure, version of the retributive theory.[7] Like other contemporary retributivists, whose views I shall examine in the following sections, Nozick believes that people deserve punishment for their wrongful acts. But he spells out the basis for deserved punishment in a different and rather striking manner by claiming that punishment is a communicative act transmitting to the wrongdoer the message showing how wrong his conduct was.

But before developing this view, Nozick usefully distin-

---

[5] See H. L. A. Hart, *Punishment and Responsibility*, p. 2 n. 3 where he refers to S. I. Benn's observation that denunciation does not imply the deliberate infliction of suffering.

[6] Ibid., p. 263.

[7] Robert Nozick, *Philosophical Explanations* (Oxford, 1981), pp. 363–97.

guishes between retributive punishment and revenge with which it is sometimes confused. (i) 'Retribution is done for a wrong, while revenge may be done for an injury or harm or slight and need not be a wrong.'[8] Later he gives an example of the distinction between a wrong and a harm by pointing out that even if the rejected suitor is harmed, no wrong has been done because the rejector had a right to reject.[9] (ii) 'Retribution sets an internal limit to the amount of punishment, according to the seriousness of the wrong, whereas revenge internally need set no limits.'[10] This is certainly true as often the person seeking revenge harms his victim until he is satisfied, and he may not be satisfied until he has inflicted much greater harm on the victim than had been inflicted by the victim on him or his loved ones. (iii) 'Revenge is personal' [11] in the sense that the revenger is the very person on whom the harm to be avenged has been inflicted, or he has a personal relationship with the person harmed. On the other hand, the dispenser of retributive punishment need not have any such personal tie with the victim of the wrongful conduct. (iv) 'Revenge involves a particular emotional tone, pleasure in the suffering of another',[12] which is missing in the case of retribution. This, according to Nozick, explains why the revenger often wishes to witness the suffering of the revengee. (v) Revenge need not be general in that it does not commit the revenger to avenging again in similar circumstances.

One other important difference between revenge and retribution, which could be added to Nozick's account, is that retributive punishment is only inflicted on the wrongdoer, whereas revenge is sometimes inflicted on an innocent person close to the revengee, either because this is an easier target, or because it is thought that this would hurt the revengee more. Thus if the revenger's mother has been harmed, he might deliberately choose to assault the revengee's mother rather than the revengee himself.

[8] Ibid., p. 366.
[9] Ibid., p. 388.
[10] Ibid., p. 367.
[11] Ibid.
[12] Ibid.

Nozick distinguishes between two types of retributivists—the teleological and the nonteleological. The teleological retributivist is a consequentionalist. The purpose of showing the offender the wrongness of his act is to bring about some further consequence, namely his moral transformation. This makes teleological retributivism into a version of the view that the purpose of punishment is to reform the offender, a view which, as we saw in the previous chapter, utilitarians accept as one of the possible beneficial consequences of punishment. Nozick does not cite any evidence to show that punishment is an effective instrument of moral transformation. This is not surprising as there is in fact very little evidence to support the view, and much evidence against it in the high rates or recidivism. However, he mentions the teleological retributivist's hope that the person who is punished for a wrongful act will realize that his act is wrong when it is done to him.[13] This of course only applies when the punishment takes the form of doing the same to the offender as he did to his victim. But even in such cases Nozick thinks that the transformation depends on the offender finding no morally relevant difference between his wrongdoing and the infliction of punishment on him.[14] But Nozick fails to see that if the offender finds no such difference, then he will treat his punishment as equally wrong! That is hardly the message that the teleological retributivist wants him to receive. So any acceptance by the offender that his punishment is justified, whereas his infliction of a similar injury on his victim is not, must rest on his recognition that there is a basis for punishment other than just to show that what he has done is wrong.

Nozick himself rejects teleological retributivism on other grounds. It will not justify punishment if there are more effective means of producing a moral transformation in the offender. It will also not justify the punishment of hardened offenders who cannot be brought to realize that they acted wrongly.

Nozick subscribes to the nonteleological version of retributivism in which punishment 'is seen as right or good in itself, apart from the further consequences to which it might

[13] Ibid., p. 372.
[14] Ibid.

lead'.[15] On this view, retributive punishment reconnects the
offender with the correct values from which his wrongdoing
has disconnected him. Through punishment the correct values
qua correct values have 'some significant effect in his life'.[16]
But Nozick does not give an adequate clarification of the central notions in his nonteological retributivism. What is it to be
'connected' with correct values, and what is meant by 'significant effect'? Most of what he says about these notions are
negative. Thus he maintains that when the correct values have
significant effect in the offender's life, this does not mean that
his conduct is guided by those values in the sense that he does
things because they are right or abstains from acts because
they are wrong.[17] Again, to be connected with correct values
is not the same as internalizing them for future action.[18]

Nozick moves towards a more positive characterization of
what it is to be connected with correct values when he writes:
'The linkage we are delineating corresponds to the recipient
of a verbal message understanding the assertion: whereas
the goal of the teleological retributivist corresponds to the
recipient's accepting what is said.'[19] But if the recipient of
retributive punishment can be connected with correct values
merely by his understanding that he is being punished because
others regard what he has done as wrong, and without his
accepting their values, then punishment has not been justified.
For we can surely ensure that the offender understands even
when the message is conveyed to him verbally in appropriately
strong terms. For example, which offender, when he is being
sternly lectured to by a moralistic judge at the sentencing
stage, can fail to understand the message? So if understanding
is all that is required, why go on to inflict punishment?

But Nozick finds a place for the suffering inflicted by punishment. It ensures that correct values have a significant effect
in people's lives, and it makes it impossible for the person who
flouts those values to remain as pleased with what he did.[20]
Suffering wipes out or weakens the wrongdoer's link with incorrect values so that he now regrets having followed those values.
But notice, he only regrets or is less pleased with his wrongful
act. Since he has not undergone a moral transformation, there

[15] Ibid., p. 374.   [16] Ibid., p. 375.   [17] Ibid., p. 377.
[18] Ibid., p. 375   [19] Ibid., p. 380.   [20] Ibid., pp. 379 and 384.

is no sense of remorse, no acceptance on his part that what he has done was wrong and not simply imprudent. There is only a realization that others regard his act as wrong and are making him suffer for it. How is this different from being deterred by punishment?

So the unfamiliar idioms that Nozick uses in expounding teleological and nonteleological retributivism seem in the end to conceal two familiar ideas; that punishment reforms, and that it deters the persons punished respectively. These ideas have only received very limited support when they were used by some utilitarians, and there is no reason to welcome their resurrection in exotic forms of retributivism.

3.4. *Punishment and Desert*

Contemporary retributivists treat the notion of desert as central to the retributive theory, punishment being justified in terms of the desert of the offender. Retributivists base their assessments of desert both on the harm done by the act, and on the mental state of the offender which determines his culpability. To be deserving of punishment the offender must be morally culpable in that his act was done in the absence of one of the accepted excuses. These excuses usually include duress, accident, reasonable mistake, and some forms of mental illness, and I shall discuss the rationale of excuses in Chapter 5. For convenience I shall use the term 'voluntary' conduct to refer to all those acts for which no excuse was available, and for which therefore a normal agent can be held morally culpable. We can then formulate retributive theories of punishment as those theories which maintain that punishment is justified because the offender has voluntarily committed a morally wrong act. Is this claim to be accepted as self-evident, or can it be supported by other considerations? How can punishment, which involves the deliberate infliction of suffering or deprivation, be justified even when it produces no good consequences such as the deterrent, reformative, and incapacitative effects which utilitarians stress?[21]

In defending the claim, retributivists divide sharply. Some have tried to justify the punishment on the ground that

---

[21] For an interesting discussion of some recent versions of retributivism, see Ted Honderich, *Punishment, The Supposed Justifications* (Harmondsworth, 1984), Postscript.

wrongdoers deserve to suffer. This appeals to a non-comparative notion of desert in which what a person deserves depends solely on what he or she has done. But other retributivists rely on comparative notions of desert, connecting punishment with more general principles of distributive justice or justice in the distribution of the benefits and burdens of social life. The offender's interests are compared respectively with those of other groups in society: the victims of crime, other offenders, and the law-abiding citizens. I shall begin by considering the view that wrongdoers deserve to suffer.

3.5. *Wrongdoers Deserve to Suffer*

In *Punishment and Desert*, Kleinig suggests that, 'The principle that wrongdoers deserve to suffer seems to accord with our deepest intuitions concerning justice.'[22] To support this claim, he cites the example of a Nazi war criminal who escapes to an uninhabited island where 30 years later he is found leading 'an idyllic existence'. While he is still unrepentant for what he has done, he has no desire to cause further harm. (Let us also assume that his punishment would have no general deterrent effect on the behaviour of others.) Kleinig thinks that the Nazi would not be justified in complaining if suffering were imposed on him for his past misdeeds, although he concedes that it is another question as to whether it would be proper for the State to inflict the suffering on him.

Kleinig's view of the Nazi is widely shared, but it is unclear what the source of the shared belief that the Nazi ought to suffer is. In many people it may be based on the desire for revenge rather than on the claims of justice. But even when it is based on considerations of justice, it may well rest, as I think it should, on a notion of comparative justice rather than on the non-comparative judgement that wrongdoers deserve to suffer. I shall return to this example in my discussion of comparative notions of desert.

Of course utilitarians do not accept Kleinig's view. For them suffering as such is bad, no matter whose suffering it is. But this too is not intuitively obvious. The disappointed sadist, racist, or Nazi suffers. The greedy and the unjust suffer when

---

[22] John Kleinig, *Punishment and Desert* (The Hague, 1973), p. 67.

they do not get other people's fair shares. We are not moved by their unhappy plight, and why should we be? We might of course believe that in a better world there would be no such people. But given that they exist, it might not be a bad thing at all that they should suffer in the ways that they do. The utilitarian will claim that this is because the elimination of their suffering will cause the greater suffering of innocent people whose misfortunes are necessary means to the alleviation of the sufferings of the wicked and the unjust. But this hardly explains why it is that if the suffering of the wicked and the unjust can be removed simply through having false beliefs about the misfortunes of the innocent, we would still feel no compulsion to encourage such false beliefs. Nor does it explain why in many contexts we simply ignore or discount their suffering as the basis of social policy.[23] For example, it would be contemptible to suggest that the fate of an innocent Jew should depend on whether giving in to the evil desires of Nazis would eliminate more suffering among otherwise disappointed Nazis than the suffering of the Jew.

So it cannot be said that at the intuitive level utilitarians have any decisive argument against Kleinig's intuitions. But whatever the intuitive force of the claim that wrongdoers deserve to suffer, it gives no support to the much stronger claim that the suffering should be deliberately inflicted by the State on wrongdoers. And it is this stronger claim which is needed to support the retributive theory of punishment. There is a familiar tradition in political philosophy which maintains that the State should prevent individuals from harming others and provide the conditions for persons to pursue their own plans of life, but that it should not seek to promote virtue or punish wrongdoing as such. Retributivists would have to develop an alternative view of the functions of the State before they could justify the punishment of wrongdoers simply on the basis of what they deserve.[24]

---

[23] See C. L. Ten, *Mill on Liberty* (Oxford, 1980), Ch. 2.

[24] This point is clearly recognized by Jeffrie G. Murphy in his brief discussion of 'the question of whether the retributivist goals, however morally admirable they may be, are *legitimate state goals*, goals that it is the state's proper business to pursue' (Murphy's emphasis). See Jeffrie G. Murphy, 'Retributivism and the State's Interest in Punishment', in J. R. Pennock and J. Chapman (eds) *Nomos XXVII: Criminal Justice* (New York, 1985), pp. 156–64.

Even if it is conceded that punishment may be imposed by the State on a wrongdoer who deserves to suffer, there is a further difficulty as to whether the deserved suffering of the wrongdoer is affected by his past undeserved suffering. If we take what Gertrude Ezorsky calls 'the whole life view' of desert, then we have to admit that a criminal does not deserve to suffer for his wrongdoing if he had, prior to the criminal offence, already suffered the appropriate amount through natural or social causes, or through being undeservedly punished for an offence he did not commit.[25] We are required to 'balance all of his moral wrongs against the suffering of his entire life'.[26]

Against this, it has been argued by W. A. Parent that the deserved suffering inflicted by punishment has an educational value which is absent in the case of suffering produced by natural or other causes.[27] But if Parent's account is accepted, then the case for punishment rests on its educational value rather than on the principle that wrongdoers deserve to suffer. So a retributivist who holds on to that principle cannot block the move to the whole-life view of desert. But once that move is made, punishment can no longer be justified on the basis of a single act of wrongdoing.

Parent also argues that desert debts and desert credits are not transferable. The offender's past suffering only alters his criminal desert if the suffering affects his ability to abstain from the criminal act. But Parent's rejection of the whole-life view of criminal desert takes us away from the apparent simplicity of the claim that wrongdoers deserve to suffer.

3.6. *Unfair to Victims*

The whole-life view of criminal desert also stands in the way of the implementation of a theory of desert which bases the offender's desert on a comparison of the relative welfare of the offender and his victim. For example, it is sometimes thought that punishment of the Nazi is justified because it is unfair that he should remain free and happy while his victims

[25] Gertrude Ezorsky, 'The Ethics of Punishment', in Gertrude Ezorsky (ed.), *Philosophical Perspectives on Punishment* (Albany, 1972), pp. xxiv–xxvi.
[26] Ibid., p. xxvi.
[27] W. A. Parent, 'The Whole Life View of Criminal Desert', *Ethics*, 86 (1976), pp. 351–3.

have perished. Punishment corrects the unjust distribution of happiness and suffering.

But here again the claim that one person has an unfair share of happiness or suffering compared to another cannot be based on the effects of a single act, but must take account of the total span of their respective lives. But if that is done, then there will be many cases in which offenders have obtained less than their fair share of happiness and their victims more than the fair share. Consider the case of a particularly deprived offender who, through no fault of his own, but as the result of social and economic circumstances beyond his control, led a very unhappy life. On the other hand, his victim is someone who, through the happy circumstances of her birth and not through any special effort on her part, had a very pleasant life until she became the victim of crime. It cannot be said that the distribution of happiness and suffering across their respective lives has been unfairly favourable to the offender and unfavourable to the victim.

In any case, it is practically impossible to apply the theory since we lack the necessary knowledge of people's lives, and any systematic attempt to acquire that knowledge will not only put an intolerable strain on the resources of the legal system, but will also be unacceptably intrusive.

3.7. *Equality of Treatment Among Offenders*

But there is a different consideration which supports the belief that the Nazi in our earlier example should be punished even though his particular punishment cannot be defended on purely utilitarian grounds. This consideration rests on a comparison of the position of the Nazi and those of other offenders who are punished for committing crimes similar to, or even much less serious than, those of the Nazi. For example, an ordinary murderer is punished for his crime. His punishment, let us assume, is justified on utilitarian grounds. Similarly there are sufficient utilitarian reasons for punishing those who have committed lesser offences like assault and theft. But if all these offenders are punished, then it is unfair that the Nazi should not also be punished for a similar, or even much worse, offence. The absence of utilitarian reasons for punishing the

Nazi arises out of circumstances which form no part of the act committed by the Nazi. Part of the appeal here is to a requirement that similar cases should be treated similarly, where the similarity is based on intrinsic features of the act, defined in terms of the intention of the agent and the natural and foreseeable consequences. This requirement of justice is not absolute, and sometimes may have to be compromised by the difficulties of enforcing the law in an imperfect world, or by other powerful utilitarian considerations. But it has some force. A related consideration is that the more serious offences should be punished more severely than the less serious ones. There is no doubt that the Nazi's crime is far graver than many other offences which are justifiably punished on utilitarian grounds.

However, the considerations cited do not in themselves dictate the punishment of the Nazi. They give rise to a conditional demand that if similar, or lesser, offenders are justifiably punished, then so must the Nazi. But whether other offenders are justifiably punished may well depend on utilitarian considerations.

3.8. *Punishment Gives Satisfactions*

Another reason why some people think that the Nazi war criminal should be punished is that his punishment brings satisfaction to others. This view has been called the satisfaction theory, and it is said to be a view that has 'given force' to retributivism.[28] But whether it can fruitfully be regarded as a retributive doctrine depends on why the fact that punishment gives satisfaction to others is regarded as something good. The Victorian judge James Fitzjames Stephen is supposed to be an advocate of the satisfaction theory when he said that the punishment of criminals gratifies 'the feeling of hatred—call it revenge, resentment, or what you will—which the contemplation of such conduct excites in healthily constituted minds'.[29] If Stephen's claim is simply that the failure to satisfy the feeling of hatred will produce socially harmful private vendettas, then his view would be straightforwardly

[28] Ted Honderich, *Punishment, The Supposed Justifications*, op. cit., p. 28. The label 'satisfaction theory' is given by John Cottingham, 'Varieties of Retribution', *The Philosophical Quarterly*, 29 (1979), pp. 241–2.
[29] Quoted by Honderich, op. cit., p. 49.

utilitarian.[30] But this is clearly not all that Stephen had in mind. There seems to be two other interpretations of why the satisfaction of the desires in question is good.

First, it might be argued that the satisfaction of *any* desire is as such good.[31] But this interpretation of the satisfaction theory transforms it into preference utilitarianism which maintains that the right course of action is that which maximizes the satisfaction of desires.[32] Now the satisfaction of all desires is relevant, no matter what their content or their source. It then becomes difficult to explain why the satisfaction theory should confine itself to the satisfactions obtained as a result of punishing offenders, and ignore other desires which punishment frustrates, including the strong desires of offenders, their families and friends against punishment.

If the satisfaction theory is to count as a retributive theory then it has to be given a different interpretation. Stephen gave a hint of an alternative interpretation when he said that the feeling of hatred is aroused in 'healthily constituted minds'. He did not therefore seem to treat the desires in question as brute facts whose presence called for satisfaction, but rather as desires of which he approved. But if we interpret the satisfaction theory in this manner, then the basis for satisfying the desire to punish the offender presumably rests on the view that the offender deserves to be punished. So the satisfaction theory cannot be used to explain the basis of the claim that the offender deserves punishment because it itself presupposes that claim.

3.9. *Unfairness to Law-Abiding Citizens*

We come now to that version of the retributive theory which justifies punishment in terms of the claim that the offender has taken an unfair advantage of the law-abiding citizens. The most well-known attempt to develop this type of retributive theory is that of Herbert Morris in his richly illuminating paper, 'Persons and Punishment'.[33] Similar theories are also

[30] See Cottingham, op. cit., p. 242.

[31] See the discussion in Honderich, op. cit., pp. 29 and 236–7.

[32] In *Mill on Liberty*, p. 36, I tried to reconstruct Stephen's view in line with his general utilitarian outlook.

[33] Herbert Morris, 'Persons and Punishment' in, Jeffrie G. Murphy (ed.), *Punishment and Rehabilitation* (Belmont, 1973). In a more recent essay, Morris argues that 'a

independently presented by John Finnis and Jeffrie Murphy.[34]

Morris maintains that 'the core rules of the criminal law', which prohibit violence and deception, confer benefits on all persons in a society. The benefits consist in the non-interference by others with a certain protected area of a person's life. But these benefits are only possible if a burden of self-restraint is accepted, and people do not seek to satisfy their inclinations to engage in activities which interfere with the protected area of the lives of others. When the criminal violates the law, he or she renounces the burden which the law-abiding citizens accept. At the same time the criminal continues to enjoy the benefits of the law. The criminal has therefore taken an unfair advantage of the law-abiding citizens.

Punishment is justified because, by removing the unfair advantage of the criminal, it restores the just equilibrium of benefits and burdens which was upset by the criminal's act. Morris goes on to argue that only those who have voluntarily renounced the relevant burden should be punished as only they have taken the unfair advantage. This provides a basis for the recognition of various legal excuses. The failure to recognize such excuses would itself produce an unfair distribution of benefits and burdens by punishing those who, although they broke the law, did so in circumstances in which they could not be said to have taken an unfair advantage.

This specifically retributive reason for punishment must be distinguished from the other reasons which Morris also mentions. Thus he claims that punishment is also justified because it prevents the weakening of the disposition to obey the law among the law-abiding citizens. If they know that offenders can renounce with impunity the burden that they have accepted, then they will be less inclined to go on accepting this burden. This reason points to the good consequences of

principal justification for punishment is the potential and actual wrongdoer's good'. See Herbert Morris, 'A Paternalistic Theory of Punishment', in Rolf Sartorius (ed.), *Paternalism* (Minneapolis, 1983).

[34] For John Finnis's contributions, see: 'Old and New in Hart's Philosophy of Punishment', *The Oxford Review*, 8 (1968); 'The Restoration of Retribution', *Analysis*, 32 (1971–2); 'Meaning and Ambiguity in Punishment (and Penology)'. *Osgooge Hall Law Journal*, 10 (1972); *Natural Law and Natural Rights* (Oxford, 1980), pp. 262–6: *Fundamentals of Ethics* (Oxford, 1983), pp. 128–32. Jeffrie G. Murphy's best known contribution is 'Marxism and Retribution' which is reprinted with other relevant essays in Jeffrie G. Murphy, *Retribution, Justice, and Therapy* (Dodrecht, 1979).

punishment in reducing crime. So also does Morris's other reason that punishment induces compliance with the rules. The specifically retributive reason, on the other hand, does not refer to the restoration of the equilibrium of the benefits and burdens as something that is distinct from, and caused by, punishment. Instead the act of punishment, by removing the unfair advantage taken by the offender, is itself the act restoring the equilibrium of benefits and burdens.

In his paper, 'The Return to Retribution in Penal Theory', D. J. Galligan distinguishes between two versions of the retributive argument for punishment.[35] The first and stronger version of the argument maintains that punishment removes the illicit advantage gained by the crime and thereby restores the equilibrium. This argument is rejected by Galligan on the ground that it fails to give an adequate explanation of how punishment restores the social equilibrium. Obviously punishment does not restore the equilibrium in the way that the repayment of a debt restores the original position. For the injury done by the crime is not removed or cancelled out by the infliction of punishment of the offender. But the second version of the argument gets round this by making no reference to the restoration of the social equilibrium as a further end to be achieved by punishment. Instead punishment is justified simply because it removes the unfair advantage which the offender has gained.

However, in Morris's account of punishment, the notion of restoring the equilibrium of benefits and burdens is not separable from the notion of removing the unfair advantage gained, or of preventing the offender from continuing to enjoy his or her illicit advantage over the law-abiding citizens. There is no further sense in which punishment is supposed to restore the social equilibrium. In other words, the equilibrium is restored not by the impossibility of wiping out what the offender has done in the past but in the very process of removing the unfair advantage gained by the offender while allowing law-abiding citizens to continue in the enjoyment of their benefits.

For Morris then the unfair advantage taken by the offender does not consist in the material benefits which the offender

[35] D. J. Galligan, 'The Return to Retribution in Penal Theory', in C. Tapper (ed.), *Crime, Proof and Punishment* (London, 1981), pp. 154–7.

might have gained, for those benefits cannot be taken back if the offender has consumed them, and has no comparable resources with which to replace them. Punishment therefore does not restore the equilibrium in the way that a tax imposed on an offender and transferred as compensation to the victim might be said to restore the equilibrium.[36] Compensation is something that is owed to victims, whereas in Morris's argument the unfairness of the offender is an unfairness to the law-abiding citizens. This means that the unfair benefit is something which the offender has, and which all the law-abiding citizens have voluntarily foregone. This benefit is the voluntary renunciation of the burden of restraining oneself from violating the law. It is this benefit which other defenders of theories similar to Morris's have identified as the relevant benefit unfairly taken by the offender. Thus Finnis speaks of the offender as having illicitly 'indulged his will', and as exercising 'self-will or free choice'.[37] And Murphy talks about the offender renouncing the burden of self-restraint.[38] So punishment removes the offender's advantage of freely indulging his or her will or of renouncing self-restraint. But it should be remembered that the indulgence of one's will or the renunciation of self-restraint only constitutes the taking of unfair advantage when it is done in the context of enjoying benefits made possible by the willingness of others to assume burdens that one has renounced.

Morris's theory of punishment seems to be a version of the more general theory of political obligation known as 'the principle of fair play' or 'the principle of fairness'. This principle, expounded in slightly different forms by Hart and Rawls, maintains that when people engage in a just and mutually beneficial joint enterprise according to rules which restrict their liberty, then those who have benefited from the submission of others to these restrictions, have a duty to submit themselves to the same restrictions.[39]

[36] See Richard Wasserstrom's discussion of his interpretation of Morris in 'Capital Punishment as Punishment: Some Theoretical Issues and Objections'. *Midwest Studies in Philosophy*, 7 (1982), p. 498.
[37] The quotations are from 'The Restoration of Retribution', p. 134, and *Natural Law and Natural Rights*, p. 263.   [38] 'Marxism and Retribution', p. 100.
[39] See: H. L. A. Hart, 'Are There Any Natural Rights?', *Philosophical Review*, 64 (1955), p. 185; and John Rawls, *A Theory of Justice* (Oxford, 1972), p. 108–14.

It is sometimes thought that this theory of political obligation has been so decisively refuted that any version of it which shares its central features cannot be taken seriously. The most well-known objections to the principle are those put forward by Nozick in *Anarchy, State, and Utopia*.[40] These objections have been subjected to detailed scrutiny by others.[41] I shall not be concerned with the merits of Nozick's objections, but I shall briefly indicate that his arguments do not affect the version of the principle of fairness that Morris needs in order to justify punishment.

Nozick gives an example of a group of people who start a public address system giving benefits in the form of playing records, telling amusing stories, and giving news bulletins. There are 365 adults in the neighbourhood, and the arrangement made by the group is that each person should spend one day running the system. If you have benefited by occasionally opening your window and listening to the entertainment, does it follow that you have a duty to play your part in running the system? Nozick argues that you have not. 'Though you benefit from the arrangement, you may know all along that 364 days of entertainment supplied by others will not be worth your giving up *one* day.'[42] You have also not consented to the scheme.

But the criminal's renunciation of the burden of self-restraint is very different from your refusal to help in the running of the public address system. In renouncing his burden, the criminal deprives law-abiding citizens of some of the benefits which he himself enjoys. Nozick's example would come closer to the case of the criminal's conduct if one supposes that for some peculiar reason your enjoyment of the public address system is enhanced by your shutting your neighbour's window thereby depriving her of the entertainment, even though, unlike you, she has already taken her turn to run the system. It is not unreasonable to claim that you have a duty to refrain from shutting her window. So Morris's theory depends on the much narrower principle that one who accepts the benefits of a just

[40] Robert Nozick, *Anarchy, State, and Utopia* (Oxford, 1974), pp. 90–5.
[41] See: A. John Simmons, *Moral Principles and Political Obligations* (Princeton, 1981), pp. 118–36; and Richard J. Arneson, 'The Principle of Fairness and Free-Rider Problems', *Ethics*, 92 (1982).   [42] *Anarchy, State and Utopia*, p. 93.

scheme of social co-operation must accept the burden of co-operation where this involves restraining oneself from depriving co-operating members of some of their benefits.

In a recent detailed criticism of Morris's theory, Richard Burgh first attributes to him the view that the offender's benefit is the sphere of non-interference resulting from general obedience to the particular law he or she violated.[43] Burgh then points out that the offender might not have benefited from the existence of that particular law. For example, embezzlers might not be in a position to be embezzled, and hence the law prohibiting embezzlement gives them no benefit. Hence they cannot be said to have taken unfair advantage of those law-abiding citizens who are in positions to be embezzled. If we shift the relevant benefit to that given by obedience to laws in general, then Burgh points out that this is a benefit which is enjoyed equally by all offenders. The murderer enjoys this benefit just as much as the embezzler. So if both of them are deserving of punishment because of the unfair benefits they have enjoyed, then both deserve punishment to the same degree. On this view there would be no basis for punishing different offenders to different degrees.

Finally, Burgh argues that the theory cannot be rescued by treating the unfair benefit of the offender as the renunciation of the burden of self-restraint. Since the extent of benefit now depends on the weight of the burden of self-restraint renounced, and the burden of self-restraint is to be measured by the strength of the inclination to commit the crime, it follows that the stronger the inclination to commit the crime, the greater is the benefit derived from the offence. But the degree of punishment suggested by this account is highly counter-intuitive, for it means that if there is a stronger inclination to evade taxes than to murder, then the punishment for tax evasion would have to be more severe than that for murder.

In fact Morris's theory combines two elements that Burgh keeps apart—the benefit of renouncing self-restraint and the benefit of obedience to laws in general. The renunciation of the burden of self-restraint is only regarded as an unfair advantage when it is done in the context of enjoying the benefits of having a protected sphere made possible by the obedience of others to laws in general. But does this interpretation still make Morris's theory vulnerable to the objections raised by Burgh that the theory either fails to account for the differential punishment to be meted out to various offenders, or that it gives a wrong account of which offender should be punished more severely?

We should recall that the offender's unfair benefits are relative to the benefits and burdens of law-abiding citizens. Any measure of the extent of the offender's benefits is a measure of the degree of unfair advantage taken, and must therefore take account of the value to both the offender and to the law-abiding citizens of the law that has been violated. For example, a petty thief, no matter what the strength of his inclination to commit the crime, still obeys the rest of the laws conferring considerable benefits on himself and the law-abiding citizens. These benefits include the protection of life which is highly valued by all parties. The murderer, on the other hand, again irrespective of the strength of his inclination to murder, violates a law which makes a far greater contribution than does the law prohibiting petty theft to the benefits enjoyed by both the murderer and law-abiding citizens. So in this sense it can be said that the unfair advantage taken by the petty thief is much less than that of the murderer. The petty thief invades a less important part of the protected sphere of others.

Morris's theory does not spell out the basis on which one is to determine the extent of punishment which each offender deserves, for it is primarily concerned with establishing a case for punishing all offenders who voluntarily invade the protected sphere. But it looks as if, contrary to Burgh's argument, it is possible to interpret the theory in a manner which makes it compatible with some proportionality principle which states that the degree of punishment should vary with the gravity of the offence committed. (I shall discuss the details of the proportionality principle in the final chapter.) Morris's theory survives so far. But there are other problems to be faced.

In the legal systems with which we are familiar, the violation of the core rules of the criminal law are met with punishments usually in the form of imprisonment and fines. But given that Morris's theory establishes the case for restoring the equilibrium of benefits and burdens by removing the unfair benefits of offenders, why is it that only these forms of punishment can remove the unfair benefits? As Galligan points out, the theory 'requires at most that the offender be singled out, condemned and subjected to some form of disadvantage; but just what manner and form the disadvantage must take is left open'.[44] Here Morris's theory needs some help from external considerations before it can provide a full justification of punishment.

The appeal to external considerations is also necessary at another point, for there are circumstances in which even offenders who have voluntarily renounced their burdens should not be punished. Finnis recognizes this when he argues that the restoration via punishment of fairness in distribution is not the only component of the social good, and so need not be pursued regardless of consequences.[45] But if utilitarian considerations enter into the final decision as to whether punishment should be inflicted, then these considerations form part of the complete theory of punishment.

For a moral pluralist, who believes in several values, each not reducible to any of the others, it makes sense to say that although fairness dictates that one should punish on a particular occasion, the requirement of fairness is overridden by other values which dictate that one should not punish. Fairness is a moral principle for guiding one's actions, and it can provide a reason for acting even when one acts against it in the light of competing reasons for action. But if fairness is only one of the considerations relevant to the determination of whether punishment should be inflicted, then fairness is not the only component of a complete theory of punishment.

So far we have acknowledged that there are considerations external to Morris's theory which count against punishing offenders who have voluntarily renounced the burden of self-restraint. But it would appear that there are also considerations internal to the theory which sometimes urge against punishment. Morris's theory treats the offender's violation of the law as the taking of an unfair advantage which punishment removes. But although punishment restores the equilibrium of benefits and burdens between the particular offender and

[44] 'The Return to Retribution in Penal Theory', p. 158.
[45] 'The Restoration of Retribution', p. 135.

the law-abiding citizens, it can also have various effects on
others. Suppose that it somehow causes others to commit
crimes. This would appear to be a relevant consideration
for *not* inflicting punishment. As Finnis acknowledges, if
punishment causes more crime, it creates greater unfairness
to law-abiding citizens, and this is surely precisely what the
theory wishes to avoid.[46] Indeed it would be odd for the theory
to insist on punishment in such a case since the people on
whose behalf punishment is exacted, namely the law-abiding
citizens, would presumably prefer a situation in which there
are fewer crimes.

But now suppose that punishment deters potential offenders
from committing crimes. Then by the same token it reduces
the unfairness to law-abiding citizens, and so the deterrent
effects of punishment should count as a reason for punishment.
In a particular case, it is possible that the punishment of an
offender will encourage some potential offenders to commit
crimes while it deters other potential offenders. If the former
effect is a reason for not punishing the offender, then the
latter effect should be a reason in favour of punishment.

But through these moves, the character of Morris's retributive theory is in danger of changing radically to the extent
that it now appears to be a type of consequentialist doctrine
which seeks to minimize unfairness or to maximize fairness.
Of course this does not mean that the doctrine collapses into
utilitarianism. Whereas utilitarianism takes into account all
the consequences of actions which affect happiness or the satisfaction of desires, the doctrine limits the relevant consequences
to those which bear on the removal of unfairness. But on this
interpretation there is now nothing in the doctrine which blocks
the punishment of the innocent if such punishment is conducive
to the minimization of unfairness. Suppose that by punishing
an innocent person we will minimize the violations of the law
and therefore the amount of unfairness. If the goal is to
minimize unfairness, then it appears that there would be no
reason to avoid such punishment. There will be no special
unfairness in punishing the innocent, for the State's punishment of the innocent is on a par with, and to be weighed on
the same scale as, the unfairness of the actions of criminals.

[46] Ibid., p. 135.

To meet this objection, it is necessary to re-examine the motivation behind Morris's theory. In fact the theory cannot be accurately represented as one which seeks to minimize unfairness by any means whatever. It starts with the assumption that it is possible to have a situation in which there is a fair distribution of benefits and burdens for everyone. Any departure from this state through the voluntary actions of individuals in renouncing their burdens while still accepting benefits is unfair, and punishment restores the initial equilibrium. So the only people who are to be punished are those who have acted unfairly. The theory is compatible with not punishing those who have acted unfairly if punishment will produce even greater unfairness. And so long as the punishment of the offender is not disproportionate to the degree of unfairness of his or her act, an appeal to other considerations can be made in order to determine the exact amount of punishment. But punishing the innocent, who have not acted unfairly, is a different matter. It strikes at the very root of the system of co-operation designed to confer equal mutual benefits on all. It means that the system itself is unfair. The system is designed to maintain fairness by punishing unfair behaviour, and not to prevent unfairness by itself sanctioning unfair acts. The aim of establishing a system of rules is to provide each person with a protected sphere in which he or she can proceed free of interference from others. The punishment of the innocent is an interference with the very area of their lives that it was the purpose of the system to protect. The system seeks to guarantee that a person will only be interfered with by the law if he or she voluntarily invades the protected sphere of others.

So in fact Morris's theory erects a barrier against punishing the innocent which resembles Nozick's idea of moral side-constraints which we are forbidden to violate even in the pursuit of desirable goals.[47] Nozick distinguishes the theory of individual rights as side-constraints from what he calls 'utilitarianism of rights'. According to the latter view, one would be required to violate a person's rights when by so doing one minimizes the total amount of violations of rights in society. So, for example, one may violate an innocent man's

[47] *Anarchy, State, and Utopia*, pp. 28–30.

right by punishing him if this will prevent a mob from rampaging through the town, killing and burning and thereby violating the rights of others. On the other hand, if rights are side-constraints, then they may not be violated even in the cause of preventing greater violations of similar rights.

There are of course also considerations external to Morris's theory which explain why it is wrong to punish the innocent. One argument deserves special mention because it relies on a feature of punishment to which we have referred earlier. Punishment expresses moral disapproval. We normally express moral disapproval for what a person has done or failed to do. But in punishing the innocent we express moral disapproval of them when there is no basis for such disapproval. All cases of punishing the innocent share this feature of unjustly attributing blame to someone who is in fact blameless. That is why such punishment is a serious wrong even when the actual suffering of deprivation inflicted by punishment may not be great in a particular case. This does not mean that it is absolutely wrong to punish the innocent. Even the idea of rights as moral side-constraints does not require that these constraints must never be violated. But it does mean that such punishment cannot be justified simply in utilitarian terms.

The scope of Morris's theory is restricted to punishment for violations of those 'core rules' of the criminal law which are necessary for the survival of society. All those living in society have a common interest in having such rules for regulating their social relations, and it is only from the application of these rules that people with otherwise very diverse interests can in principle gain equal benefits and share equal burdens. The general content of these rules depends on facts about human nature and the natural world. Morris himself draws attention to some of these facts in the following remark: 'Let us suppose that men are constituted roughly as they now are, with rough equivalence in strength and abilities, a capacity to be injured by each other and to make judgements that such injury is undesirable, a limited strength of will, and a capacity to reason and to conform conduct to rules.'[48] Hart has a more detailed discussion in his account of 'the minimum content of

[48] 'Persons and Punishment', p. 42.

natural law'.[49] The additional features on which Hart focuses are limited resources, and the need for division of labour to ensure efficient production. The vulnerability of human beings to injury means they require protection by rules prohibiting assault and killing. Limited resources mean that if individuals are to have incentives to cultivate these resources for food, there must be rules protecting food from being taken while it is in the process of cultivation. Rules protecting property are therefore necessary, although the exact content of these rules will vary from society to society. Division of labour leads to exchange of goods and thus calls for rules regulating such exchanges. There will be a common interest in protection against fraud.

Morris's theory will not therefore be relevant to all the cases in which punishment may be thought to be justified. One such case, cited by Burgh, is the law prohibiting cruelty to animals.[50] This limitation in its scope is not fatal to the theory, but it shows, what should by now be obvious, that there are other reasons for justifying the punishment which are not captured by the theory. Even within the area of its application the theory cannot possibly tell the full story about the wrongness of, for example, murder and assault. For the theory locates the wrongness of such acts in the unfairness to law-abiding citizens, and not in the harm inflicted on victims.

There is a more general problem about the application of Morris's theory to societies in the real world which all deviate in varying degrees from the ideal of a just society. Finnis makes explicit his supposition that 'the legal system and social order in question are substantially just . . . '[51] But Murphy points out that the theory is largely inapplicable to contemporary societies where there are vast inequalities of income, wealth, and opportunities.[52] In these societies most criminals come from economically and socially disadvantaged groups which cannot be said to derive much benefit from the operation of the rules of society. Morris's theory presupposes a just equilibrium of benefits and burdens which the criminal's act upsets,

---

[49] H. L. A. Hart, *The Concept of Law* (Oxford, 1961), pp. 189–95.
[50] 'Do the Guilty Deserve Punishment?', p. 205.
[51] *Natural Law and Natural Rights*, p. 264.
[52] 'Marxism and Retribution'.

and which is then restored by punishment. But if Murphy is right, then the distribution of social benefits and burdens is in the first place unfair, and punishment does not therefore restore fairness. Even if we confine the relevant burden to self-restraint, it is quite clear that the economically and socially favoured groups in society will find it much easier to accept the burden of self-restraint than disadvantaged groups.

So if criminals were all the victims of a broader social injustice in the distribution of society's resources, and the victims of crime were all the beneficiaries of the injustice, then Morris's theory would have no application. But the situation is in fact more complex. Many of the victims of crime come from the same economically and socially deprived groups as those who offend against them and there is also a substantial number of offenders who belong to the favoured groups in society. So even in societies in which the distribution of benefits and burdens is quite unfair, the argument that crime involves the taking of an unfair advantage from law-abiding citizens still has some residual force. Of course the problems of general social injustice cannot be solved by punishment.

Secondly, not to punish offenders will very likely result in even greater injustice. It will encourage more crime and lead to attempts at private enforcement of rules. The passion for revenge will remain unchecked. There will be a profusion of vigilante groups whose attitudes towards criminals will be quite brutal. And those most likely to suffer will be the poor and disadvantaged who are unable to protect themselves as well as others.

But Morris's theory runs into further difficulties because it seems to rest on dubious psychological assumptions. Self-restraint, exercised in conforming to the law, is seen as a burden which some accept for the benefit of all, while others reject it. However, many, and perhaps most, law-abiding citizens lack the desire to violate the core rules of the criminal law in the first place. For them conformity with the law does not involve the acceptance of the burden of self-restraint. Other law-abiding citizens have to exercise self-restraint in not breaking the law, but they refrain from breaking the law out of the fear of punishment rather than out of a desire to maintain the system of mutually beneficial social co-operation. Offenders cannot be said to have taken unfair advantage of these law-abiding citizens who would themselves be offenders but for the deterrent effect of punishment.[53]

Our discussion of retributive theories suggests that on their own these theories provide inadequate justifications of punishment. For even when they succeed in showing that some form of action should be taken against offenders, they do not explain why such action should take the specific form of punishment. There are a number of options open of which punishment is only one. The selection of punishment itself, or a particular form of punishment, from the available options is based on the utilitarian consideration that the practice of punishment is in general most effective in reducing crime. But once punishment is chosen as the preferred general response to crime, retributive considerations can provide further support for the punishment of offenders in particular cases. Retributive considerations also shape the practice of punishment by imposing strong constraints on the punishment of the innocent.

[53] I owe these points to discussion with H. L. A. Hart but he is not responsible for the manner in which I have formulated or used them.

4

THE SCOPE AND WEIGHT OF REASONS FOR
PUNISHMENT

4.1. *Introduction*

UTILITARIAN and retributive theories of punishment provide different reasons for justifying punishment. To what extent, if at all, are these reasons compatible with each other? This depends on the scope of application of the theories and their respective weights. Considerations of scope refer to the range of cases that utilitarian and retributive reasons are meant to cover, whereas considerations of weight refer to the strength of those reasons in cases where they do apply. If two reasons apply to different cases, then they do not conflict. Some attempts to reconcile utilitarian and retributive theories of punishment narrow the scope of application of the theories in such a manner that they no longer conflict. Other attempts at reconciliation depend on the respective weights to be given to utilitarian and retributive reasons for punishment, or invoke both considerations of scope and weight to effect the reconciliation.

Retributivists believe that a retributive reason for punishment is at least a good reason for punishment, that is a reason, which in the absence of reasons against punishment, would justify punishment. But of course good reasons for action may conflict, and the presence of a good reason may not be sufficient for action. Retributivists can therefore disagree among themselves about whether retributive reasons for punishment merely provide one basis for punishment which can be outweighed by non-retributive considerations, or whether retributive reasons are on their own always sufficient to justify punishment. Again they may disagree about whether retributive reasons are necessary for justifiable punishment in the sense that unless there is a retributive basis for punishment, punishment is never justified.

It will be evident from our discussion in Chapter 2 that the utilitarian theory of punishment applies to all cases of punishment. It lays down both necessary and sufficient conditions for the justification of punishment. So unless the theory is amended, there is no scope for reconciling it with retributive theories in so far as these latter theories maintain that some form of moral desert is either a necessary or a sufficient condition for punishment. From the utilitarian point of view, moral desert cannot be a necessary condition for justifying punishment because if the best consequences are produced by punishing the innocent, or others who do not deserve punishment, then punishment is still justified: utilitarian considerations are sufficient. Moral desert also cannot be a sufficient reason because it would not justify punishment unless punishment also produces the best consequences: utilitarian considerations are necessary. Can desert provide at least a good reason for punishment? For the utilitarian, the answer is again 'No', because the only good reasons for punishment have to do with the consequences of such punishment. In so far as moral desert embodies reasons for punishment which are independent of the desirable consequences of punishment, moral desert cannot be a good reason for punishment.

4.2. Rawls and Rule-Utilitarianism

So it would appear that the comprehensive scope of the utilitarian theory and its exclusion of non-utilitarian reasons for punishment preclude any compromise between the theory and retributive theories. But attempts have been made to narrow the scope of the utilitarian theory. The most well-known attempt is that of Rawls in his paper, 'Two Concepts of Rules'.[1]

Rawls distinguishes between, on the one hand, the justification of a rule, or a practice consisting of a system of rules, or an institution, and, on the other hand, the justification of a particular act falling under a rule or practice or institution. Thus we can distinguish between the general rule that one ought to keep one's promises and the particular act of Alice

---

[1] John Rawls, 'Two Concepts of Rules', in H. B. Acton (ed.), *The Philosophy of Punishment* (London, 1969). Excerpts from the paper are also reprinted under the title 'Punishment as a Practice' in Jeffrie G. Murphy (ed.), *Punishment and Rehabilitation* (Belmont, 1973).

keeping her promise to Bob today. Rawls points out that whereas the legislator is concerned with the justification of practices or institutions, the judge is concerned with the impartial application to particular cases of the rules made by the legislator. The ideal legislator would be a utilitarian who chooses between alternative institutions on the basis of their contributions to furthering the interests of society. The judge, on the other hand, justifies the punishment of particular offenders on the retributive basis that they are guilty of breaking legal rules. Rawls thus reconciles the utilitarian theory with the retributive theory by assigning them to different levels of justification and thus avoiding conflicts between them.

Rawls believes that by this modification of utilitarianism he succeeds in avoiding the objection to the utilitarian theory that it justifies the punishment of the innocent in appropriate circumstances. He asks us to imagine an institution, which he calls that of 'telishment', which authorizes officials to exercise their discretion in arranging a trial to condemn an innocent person whenever they think that this would be in the best interest of society.[2] Now suppose that a legislator has to choose between this institution of telishment and the alternative institution of punishment in which punishment is only permitted for the proven violation of properly promulgated, prospective legal rules.

Rawls argues that, on utilitarian grounds, the institution of punishment is to be preferred to that of telishment. For if we have the institution of telishment, then we run the risk that officials will abuse their discretionary powers, and innocent people will be fearful of becoming the victims of these officials. But once the institution of punishment has been adopted, the rules of that institution prohibit officials from exercising discretion to punish an innocent person even when this will produce the best overall consequences. Rawls's position, which limits the utilitarian justification to the level of rules, practices, or institutions, is often called rule-utilitarianism as opposed to act-utilitarianism which is the version of utilitarianism we discussed in Chapter 2. The act-utilitarian applies the utilitarian principle to every act, and on that basis, justifies an act if and only if it produces the best consequences relative to alternative acts. The rule-utilitarian requires that we perform every act which falls under the best rule, where what counts as the best rule is the rule which has the best utilitarian justification. A rule-utilitarian can therefore acknowledge that there are particular cases in which punishing innocent persons will be optimific, but, unlike the act-utilitarian, he will still insist that such punishments are wrong if they violate the rulers of the best institution.

To be a distinctive doctrine, rule-utilitarianism must not collapse into a form of sophisticated act-utilitarianism.[3] An act-utilitarian will recognize that for a variety of reasons we should not always calculate the relative consequences of performing each particular act or its alternatives, but often have to rely on general rules.[4] We know from experience that in most situations abiding by proven rules, like keeping one's promises or telling the truth, would be justified on act-utilitarian grounds. So unless a case arises which is rather untypical, the act-utilitarian will tend to assume that the consequences of keeping one's promises or telling the truth on a particular occasion are likely to be the same as those in the majority of cases. So he will do what the relevant rule requires of him. That does not make him into a rule-utilitarian. In everyday life we may lack the knowledge or the time to work out the consequences of particular actions. We may also make mistakes in our calculation. For example, if breaking our promise will be in our best interests on a particular occasion, we may tend to overlook or play down the bad consequences to others of breaking the promise. Sticking to the rule will free us from the temptation to partiality towards our own interests. But in all these cases, the act-utilitarian acts in accordance with rules only because he has good reason to believe that in so acting he is likely to produce the best consequences on the particular occasion.

So the difference between the act-utilitarian and the rule-utilitarian is not that the latter regards rules as important

---

[3] See the discussion in David Lyons, *Forms and Limits of Utilitarianism* (Oxford, 1965).

[4] See, for example, J. J. C. Smart, 'Extreme and Restricted Utilitarianism', in Michael D. Bayles (ed.), *Contemporary Utilitarianism* (New York, 1968), pp. 104–7. 'Extreme utilitarianism' is the same as act-utilitarianism, and 'restricted utilitarianism' is the same as rule-utilitarianism.

whereas the former regards acts as important. In general there is no conflict between these two attitudes. If there is a genuine difference between act- and rule-utilitarianism, then it must lie in the fact that there are situations in which they will act differently. But this can only be so if on those occasions the rule-utilitarian requires one to act in a manner that will not in fact produce the best consequences. Let us therefore assume that a situation arises in which the legal officials of Rawls's institution of punishment *know* that by punishing an innocent man the best consequences will be produced. We shall also assume that the officials can successfully deceive the general public into believing that the man is guilty, and that the deception will not be found out. Under these circumstances the act-utilitarian will justify the punishment of the innocent man even though the punishment is illegal. But the rule-utilitarian will regard the action as wrong because it is a violation of the rules of the institution of punishment. But why would anyone, motivated solely by utilitarian considerations, act in accordance with a rule even on those rare occasions when it is known that obeying the rule will fail to produce the best consequences? The answer cannot be that in the overwhelming majority of cases obeying the rule will produce the best consequences. The answer will only be acceptable if the case at hand is relevantly similar to those other cases. But *ex hypothesi* it is different. The rule-utilitarian has been accused of 'rule worship', of blind conformity to a generally useful rule even when he knows that obeying the rule on a particular occasion will have worse consequences than breaking the rule.[5] This accusation has some force if the rule was adopted for purely utilitarian reasons, and that is the assumption that Rawls wants us to accept. For if your only reason for telling the truth is that it is optimific, then you will have no good reason for telling the truth in a situation in which it will produce very bad consequences. But of course your commitment to telling the truth may be partly independent of the consequences produced by the act, and this commitment may lead you to act in a manner similar to the rule-utilitarian. But you will not then be motivated solely by utilitarian considerations. So in

[5] Ibid., p. 199.

so far as Rawls's theory commits him to not punishing the innocent even in situations in which the act-utilitarian will do so, then his commitment is partly at least to non-utilitarian values, or else would appear to be a form of irrational rule worship.[6]

The choice which Rawls presents between the institution of punishment and that of telishment is unnecessarily restrictive from the utilitarian point of view. It may indeed be the choice that the legislator has to make. But once the legislator has established the institution of punishment, the utilitarian judge is not committed to blindly following the rules of the institution. In deciding how to act, the utilitarian judge will of course have to take account of the effects of his or her actions on the useful institution of punishment itself. But the utilitarian's ultimate commitment transcends the commitments of his or her institutional role to obey the rules of the institution of punishment. This ultimate commitment to producing the best consequences will sometimes require the utilitarian officials to violate the rules of the institution.

Rawls therefore fails to explain why the utilitarian would be motivated to adopt rule-utilitarianism rather than act-utilitarianism. In Chapter 2 I argued for the modification of act-utilitarianism in order to give independent weight to distributive considerations, and especially to the avoidance of punishing the innocent for the benefit of the rest of society. I shall now consider whether retributive reasons for punishment, if adjusted in their scope and weight, can be made compatible with a modified act-utilitarianism.

4.3. *The Scope and Weight of Retributive Theories*

The scope of application of retributive reasons for punishment creates a problem for some retributivists who think that moral wrongdoers as such deserve to suffer by being punished. But if this is correct then it would seem to follow that punishment is justified not just for illegal acts which are morally wrong, but also for morally wrong acts which are not legally

---

[6] 'Two Concepts of Rules' was published much earlier than Rawls's deservedly celebrated book *A Theory of Justice* (Oxford, 1972) which puts forward a non-utilitarian theory of distributive justice. This book contains many important objections to utilitarianism.

proscribed. Thus we know that whereas there is an overlap between immorality and crime, not all acts of immorality are criminal. Nor indeed are all criminal acts necessarily immoral. The State would not be justified in punishing moral wrong-doers whose acts are legal. On the other hand, to restrict the justification of punishment to illegal acts, irrespective of the moral quality of these acts, would also sever the link between punishment and moral wrongdoing which lies at the heart of retributive theories.

C. W. K. Mundle, who sees the difficulties clearly, paves a middle path between these two views by suggesting that punishment by the State is justified if a person commits an act which is both a legal and a moral offence.[7] This view relies on the assumption that we have an obligation to obey the law which is based on the fact that the law's regulation of our conduct is a necessary condition of civilized life. Mundle points out that his retributive theory permits the punishment not only of those acts which are intrinsically morally wrong, but also of acts which are in themselves morally neutral. Thus traffic rules do not proscribe intrinsically wrong acts, but given that there is a moral obligation to obey the law, the violation of traffic rules is morally wrong.

Mundle gives no account of what sorts of acts would be morally wrong. As a limiting case, could one consistently adopt a utilitarian criterion of moral wrongness, and then combine it with a retributive theory of punishment? This would appear to be possible because, unlike utilitarianism which applies to all acts and not just to acts of punishment, the retributive theory is just a theory of punishment. If a retributivist adopts a utilitarian criterion of moral wrongness to identify the sorts of acts which should be subjected to punishment, it does not follow that the retributive theory of punishment will itself collapse into the act-utilitarian theory, although it will resemble some form of rule-utilitarianism. From the purely act-utilitarian point of view, the fact that an act is morally wrong does not entail that it should be punished. Every act should be judged by its consequences, and the consequences

[7] C. W. K. Mundle, 'Punishment and Desert', in H. B. Acton (ed.), *The Philosophy of Punishment* (London, 1969), p. 78.

of performing an act are not necessarily the same as the consequences of punishing someone for the performance of that act. On the other hand, the retributivist who adopts a utilitarian criterion of moral wrongness while still clinging on to the retributive theory of punishment, will presumably justify punishment in terms of the past act of wrongdoing rather than the desirable future effects of punishment.

But is such a retributive doctrine really coherent? The retributivist will have to explain why the justification of punishment should not also be determined by the utilitarian criterion which is applied to other actions. Perhaps the consistency of the retributive doctrine can be secured by distinguishing between different levels of actions: what counts as wrongdoing is one thing, and how one should treat wrongdoers is a different thing. An analogy might be drawn at this point with the distinction that is sometimes made between for example the reasons for making promises and the reasons for keeping promises.[8] Promises may be made for purely self-interested reasons or for utilitarian considerations, but irrespective of one's reasons for making promises, one has an obligation to keep one's promises. On one view, one's obligation to keep one's promises depends on a fact about the past, that one has made a promise, and is independent of facts about the future effects of keeping one's promise. But this analogy is inappropriate. In the case of promising there is a clear distinction between explanation and justification. Self-interest or utilitarian considerations explain the making of promises, but, on the view we are discussing one's obligation to keep the promise depends on the fact that one has made it. On the other hand, in the case of punishment, actions at both levels have to be justified.

In a retributive theory like Herbert Morris's, the relevant wrongdoing is the taking of an unfair advantage for oneself thereby upsetting the just equilibrium of benefits and burdens. But I have suggested in the previous chapter that the scope of Morris's theory should only extend to the punishment of those who violate rules which are necessary for the survival

---

[8] For example, in *The Logic of Leviathan* (Oxford, 1969), David P. Gauthier points out that '. . . the grounds on which we oblige ourselves do not themselves determine the character of our obligation. An obligation undertaken for prudential reasons is no less a moral obligation than one undertaken for moral reasons.' (p. 93.)

of society, for it is only those rules which can confer equal benefits on all. The scope of the theory does not therefore cover all cases in which punishment is thought to be justified.

There is an important question here about the type of conduct for which punishment is justified, and this is related to the problem of the limits of the State's proper function. In his essay *On Liberty*, John Stuart Mill gave his famous answer in terms of what he called his 'one very simple principle':

> That principle is, that the sole end for which mankind are warranted, individually or collectively, in interfering with the liberty of action of any of their number, is self-protection. That the only purpose for which power can be rightfully exercised over any member of a civilised community against his will, is to prevent harm to others. His own good, either physical or moral, is not a sufficient warrant. He cannot rightfully be compelled to do or forbear because it will be better for him to do so, because it will make him happier, because, in the opinions of others, to do so would be wise, or even right.[9]

The principle is in fact rather complex, and the whole issue of what sorts of acts may legitimately be punished by the State is too large to be discussed here.[10] I shall however assume that it is improper for the State to punish conduct which is not harmful and is merely regarded as immoral by the majority in society, or by any other group. I shall also assume that it is wrong for the State to punish a person's voluntary actions which harms no one but the agent himself or herself in situations in which the agent is aware of the harmful nature of the actions, or of the risks that harm might ensue. I shall therefore assume that punishment by the State is only justified when the scope of conduct to be punished does not extend to such cases, and this is a limitation on the State's power which any retributive or utilitarian theory of punishment must accommodate.

But even if we can get agreement about the scope of their theory, retributivists may still disagree about the weight of

---

[9] John Stuart Mill, *On Liberty in Utilitarianism, Liberty, Representative Government* (Everyman edn., London, 1910), pp. 72–3.
[10] But see C. L. Ten, *Mill on Liberty* (Oxford, 1980).

the theory. Here we have strong and weak versions of the retributive theory. An uncompromisingly strong version of the retributive theory is supposed to be exemplified in this quotation from Kant:

Even if a civil society were to dissolve itself by common agreement of all its members (for example, if the people inhabiting an island decided to separate and disperse themselves around the world), the last murderer remaining in prison must first be executed, so that everyone will duly receive what his actions are worth and so that the bloodguilt thereof will not be fixed on the people because they failed to insist on carrying out the punishment; for if they fail to do so, they may be regarded as accomplices in this public violation of legal justice.[11]

This passage has often been interpreted to mean that punishment, in this case the execution of the murderer, is required even though no good consequences will be produced.[12] Interpreted in this manner, Kant can be said to subscribe to a very strong retributive theory which maintains that the voluntary commission of a morally wrong act is both a necessary and sufficient condition of the legal authority's duty to punish the offender. On this view, punishment is justified in the sense that it is required or obligatory. Such a very strong retributive theory is not plausible because, if indeed the legal authority has an absolute duty to punish, then it follows that punishment is required even when disastrous consequences will come about, even 'when the skies will fall'. For example, suppose that the punishment of an offender will lead to a vast increase in violent crime which will terrorize law-abiding citizens who would all much prefer that the punishment not be meted out. The theory would still insist on punishment. It is a strange notion of justice whose demands benefit nobody, and whose execution will keep even the virtuous and innocent awake with fear and trembling.

[11] Immanuel Kant, 'The Right to Punish', in Jeffrie G. Murphy (ed.), *Punishment and Rehabilitation* (Belmont, 1973), p. 37. This is an excerpt from Kant's *The Metaphysical Elements of Justice*, translated by John Ladd (Indianapolis, 1965).
[12] However, John Cottingham has argued that Kant is appealing here to 'unmistakably consequentialist' considerations, namely that punishment placates God's anger and thereby prevents disastrous consequences. See his 'Varieties of Retribution', in *The Philosophical Quarterly*, 29 (1979), pp. 243–4.

However, punishment can be said to be justified, not in the sense that it is morally required, but in the sense that it is morally permissible. We will then get another, and still quite strong, version of the retributive theory which states that the voluntary commission of a morally wrong act is both a necessary and sufficient condition of the legal authority being morally permitted, or having the right to punish the offender.[13] This theory allows the legal authority not to punish the offender when such punishment will not produce good consequences, or worse, will produce disastrous consequences. So the weight of the retributive reason for punishment is reduced when the theory creates a right to punish offenders rather than imposes a moral requirement that offenders should be punished. A compromise with utilitarianism seems possible if the theory goes on to claim that the right to punish should only be exercised when by so doing the best consequences will be produced.

But now, if the mere voluntary commission of a morally wrong act is indeed both a necessary and sufficient condition of the moral permissibility of punishment, then it follows that the legal authority has not acted wrongly when it chooses to punish the offender even in situations when disastrous consequences will follow. No doubt the exercise of the right to punish may in some circumstances be 'foolish or mean',[14] but in the present context it would appear that the constraints on not acting foolishly or meanly are not moral constraints on punishment, but non-moral constraints. Thus someone could have the right to get married, but it would be foolish for her to marry a particular man who will make her unhappy. Or I have the right to spend my money on a good holiday, but it would be mean of me not to lend some of it to my friend who has overspent his own money on a very good holiday. On the other hand if the constraints are moral, then the theory is incomplete, and the right to punish which it creates is only a *prima facie* right which it would be wrong to exercise in certain situations. The retributive theory would not then lay down

[13] K. G. Armstrong, 'The Retributivist Hits Back', in H. B. Acton (ed.), *The Philosophy of Punishment* (London, 1969), pp. 155–7. Armstrong argues that one reason for the dismissal of the retributive theory is the false belief that the theory makes it an 'inescapable obligation' to inflict pain when what the theory in fact does is to create a right to inflict pain.

[14] Ibid., p. 157.

necessary and sufficient conditions for the justification of punishment.

Let us now consider two weaker versions of the retributive theory. The first regards retributive reasons as sufficient, but not necessary, for justifiable punishment, while the second maintains that retributive reasons are necessary, but not sufficient, for justifiable punishment.

In the paper discussed earlier, Mundle entertains, but does not himself endorse, the view that retributive and utilitarian considerations each provides a sufficient reason for justifiable punishment.[15] He points out that a similar view has been suggested by A. G. N. Flew. Flew argues that there is no inconsistency in justifying punishment with both utilitarian and retributive reasons.[16] Indeed there is no inconsistency if all that Flew means is that retributive and utilitarian reasons are each good, but neither is necessary nor sufficient. But the section under which Flew conducts this discussion is headed 'Overdetermination', and this seems to suggest the view that Mundle attributes to him, namely that there are multiple justifications of punishment, each of which would be sufficient. Is the justification of punishment overdetermined in the sense in which the cause of the death of a person, who has been shot through the head and just before dying is run over by a lorry, is overdetermined? Each cause of death is sufficient, but neither is necessary. But such a view of punishment, even though it can be stated in a consistent manner, would be very strange indeed. It would combine the faults of the more usual forms of retributive and utilitarian theories. For if a utilitarian justification of punishment is sufficient, then we are justified in punishing the innocent when the consequences of such punishment are optimific. On the other hand, if the retributive justification of punishment is also sufficient, then the punishment of the guilty would be acceptable even if it led to disaster. A theory with such a multiplicity of unacceptable implications cannot surely be what Flew has in mind. Flew wants to avoid 'a single unitary and comprehensive justification for all justified punishments',[17] and this perhaps only commits him to

---

[15] 'Punishment and Desert', pp. 80–1.

[16] Antony Flew, 'The Justification of Punishment', in H. B. Acton (ed.), *The Philosophy of Punishment* (London, 1969), p. 101.　　　　　　[17] Ibid., p. 101.

finding room in his theory of punishment for both retributive
and utilitarian considerations without giving either of them
the weight of sufficient reasons.

In any case there does not seem to be much point in holding
on to the view that the retributive reasons for punishment are
sufficient. For, since retributive reasons are not regarded as
necessary, this view sets up no barrier against the punishment
of the innocent. At the same time it also prevents even the
strongest utilitarian reasons against punishment from outweighing the retributive case for punishment. Of course no
retributivist worth his salt would be prepared to allow a very
minor utilitarian reason against punishment to outweigh the
retributive reason for punishment. But to acknowledge this
fact is only to recognize that retributive reasons for punishment
have some weight, are good reasons, and not that they are
sufficient reasons for punishment.

Let us now turn to the second version of the weak retributive
theory which treats retributive reasons as necessary but not
sufficient for the justification of punishment. This captures the
concern of the retributivist that the innocent should not be
punished. At the same time it leaves room for a compromise
with utilitarianism which would capture what for many are
the more attractive features of each theory. Such a Compromise
Theory can be stated as follows:

Punishing a person is justified if and only if:
(i) he is an offender who has voluntarily violated a legiti-
    mate law; (Retributive Condition), and
(ii) punishing him is justified on utilitarian grounds; (Utili-
    tarian Condition).

By a 'legitimate law' I mean a law that falls within the proper
concerns of the State. In my earlier brief allusion to the limits
of the State's function, I said that justifiable punishment should
be restricted to certain types of conduct, and the reference
here to 'legitimate law' is meant to satisfy that general condition, the details of which require much more discussion than
I have been able to give here.

The Compromise Theory meets most of the objections that
have been raised against retributive and utilitarian theories.
It makes the Retributive Condition independent of the Utilita-

rian Condition. Both conditions enter into the justification of every case of punishment. Each condition is necessary, and the two conditions are jointly sufficient for the justification of punishment.

The theory is attractive and can be applied to most situations. But in the light of our earlier discussion, it is clear that the Compromise Theory is too rigid since both the Retributive and Utilitarian Conditions admit of a few exceptions. It is unjust to punish the innocent, and this injustice normally outweighs the gain in benefits which such punishment may yield. But any pluralistic theory of punishment, which recognizes several independent values which may conflict, cannot absolutely rule out the small sacrifice of one value for a big gain in another value. So, for example, we will be confronted with an exception to the Retributive Condition if the relatively minor punishment of an innocent person is the only way to prevent grave harm to other innocent persons as a result of increased crime. But it is not enough that the aggregate harm that others are spared through the punishment of one innocent person should exceed, even by a large amount, the harm of punishment, for each of the others may only be slightly harmed if there are many of them. Punishing the innocent is also particularly unjust because it involves the moral condemnation of a blameless person for the benefit of others, and this injustice carries a weight over and above the suffering inflicted by punishment. So we need something like the following general exception to the Retributive Condition:

> Punishing an innocent person would be justified if and only if punishing him inflicts much less suffering on him than the suffering that at least one other innocent person would have experienced as an additional victim of crime had there been no punishment.

A pluralistic theory of punishment, which gives some independent weight to retributive considerations, would also qualify the Utilitarian Condition. We have in the previous chapter discussed the case of the Nazi, with personal responsibility to the execution of many Jews, and I argued for his punishment even though no overall utilitarian purpose is thereby served.

The case for punishment here is particularly strong if such punishment does not have other serious adverse effects on non-offenders. At the end of Chapter 2, I also indicated that not all cases in which punishment is thought to be justified are cases in which the existing evidence indicates that such punishment will produce consequences outweighing the suffering caused by punishment. There may be insufficient evidence to justify punishment on purely utilitarian grounds, and the Utilitarian Condition is therefore not satisfied. But in such cases retributive considerations may tip the scales in favour of punishment if there are similar or lesser offences whose punishment is justified on utilitarian grounds. From a retributivist point of view it would be unfair to punish an offender for a lesser offence and yet not punish another offender for a more serious offence. So given that the lesser offender is to be punished for utilitarian reasons, the more serious offender should also be punished though not on utilitarian grounds. It therefore appears that the exception to the Utilitarian Condition can be stated as follows:

> Punishing someone who is guilty of voluntarily committing a serious offence is justified even though it is not optimific, provided that the punishment does not have further serious adverse effects on others, and that those guilty of similar or lesser offences are punished for utilitarian reasons.

We can now incorporate the two exceptions into a Revised Compromise Theory which states that punishing a person is justified if and only if:

(i) he is an offender who has voluntarily violated a legitimate law, or an innocent person whose punishment will inflict much less suffering on him than the suffering that at least one other innocent person would have experienced as an additional victim of crime had there been no punishment; and

(ii) punishing him does not have serious adverse effects on others, and punishing those who have voluntarily committed similar or lesser offences is justified on utilitarian grounds.

Although the cases of punishing the innocent that have been

discussed so far refer to non-offenders, the notion of an 'innocent person' should be taken in a wider sense to refer to blameless offenders as well, that is to those who have an excuse
which would normally exempt them from any punishment. In
practice it is likely that such blameless offenders are the only
innocent persons whose punishment on rare occasions would
satisfy the conditions laid down in the theory. I shall discuss
the position of these offenders in the next chapter.

It remains to compare the Revised Compromise Theory
with the well-known theory of punishment enunciated by
H. L. A. Hart.

4.4. *Hart's Theory*

Hart argues that the justification of punishment raises a
number of different issues, and any account which gives a
single answer—whether it be the pursuit of a single value or
a plurality of values—to a single question is inadequate.[18] We
have instead to look for different answers to different questions.
Hart distinguishes between three such questions: (i) what justifies the general practice of punishment? (ii) who may be
punished? (iii) how severely may we punish? The first question
is about the General Justifying Aim of punishment, while the
second and third questions are about its Distribution which
has two aspects: (a) Liability (Who may be punished?) and
(b) Amount (How severely may we punish?).[19]

Hart maintains that the General Justifying Aim of punishment is the utilitarian one of protecting society from the harm
caused by crime, and not the Retributive aim of inflicting pain
on offenders who are morally guilty. But he points out that
the pursuit of the General Justifying Aim has to be qualified
by principles of justice which restrict the application of punishment to only those who have voluntarily broken the law. He
also believes that the Amount of punishment is only partly
determined by the General Justifying Aim and partly by other
considerations. But this is an issue the discussion of which I
shall postpone to the last chapter. In the remainder of this

---

[18] H. L. A. Hart, *Punishment and Responsibility* (Oxford, 1968) p. 3. For the present
discussion, the most relevant essay in Hart's book is the first essay, 'Prolegomenon
to the Principles of Punishment'.

[19] Ibid., pp. 3–4, 8–13.

chapter I shall concentrate on only part of Hart's case for the principles of justice—that part which prohibits the punishment of those who have not breached the rules laid down in the criminal law. Hart's account of the principles of justice is of course broader, restricting punishment to those who have voluntarily broken the law, thereby also excluding offenders who have an excuse. I shall discuss in greater detail Hart's rationale of legal excuses in the next chapter.

Hart makes a number of important points about the relation between the General Justifying Aim and the Distribution of punishment. First, he maintains that the principles of justice, which apply to the Distribution of punishment, are not derivable from either Utilitarianism or Retributivism in the General Justifying Aim. They represent independent values which may sometimes conflict with Utilitarianism that Hart accepts as the General Justifying Aim of punishment. In this respect Hart's theory is different from Rawls's rule-utilitarianism which tries to show that the punishment of the innocent is not justified because the utilitarianly justified practice of punishment prohibits such punishment. Rawls distinguishes between different levels in a theory of punishment but believes that ultimately punishment is justified in terms of a single value, utilitarianism. Hart, on the other hand, maintains that there are a number of different issues in the justification of punishment, and there is no single value which can properly account for all the features of punishment that require justification. But Hart believes that although the principles of justice are independent of and sometimes conflicting with Utilitarianism, their restriction of punishment to those who have voluntarily broken the law does not refute Utilitarianism as the General Justifying Aim of punishment.

Hart sometimes refers to the principles of justice as retribution in Distribution, but he is careful to point out that these principles can be defended without having to embrace the view that the General Justifying Aim of the practice of punishment is Retribution. In this he is right, for the principles of justice do not justify any specific rules or set of rules. They are therefore to be distinguished from, for example, the principle of fairness discussed in the previous chapter, which is used to justify the core rules of the criminal law which ideally create an equilibrium of equal benefits and burdens. So the application of the principles of justice does not in any way vindicate a particular set of rules. The breach of a morally evil law does not entail that the offender is morally guilty, but if the evil law is applied even to those who have not voluntarily broken it, then this is an added wrong inflicted by the law.[20]

But although the application of the principles of justice (or retribution in Distribution) does not entail Retribution as the General Justifying Aim, it does constrain, without nullifying, the pursuit of utilitarian goals as the General Justifying Aim of punishment. The principles of justice are meant to ensure that in the pursuit of general social aims like preventing crime, justice or fairness to individuals is not sacrificed. It is unfair to use individuals as a means for promoting beneficial social consequences unless they have the capacity and fair opportunity to ensure their behaviour conforms to the demands of the law.[21] Without the constraints of the principles of justice, the pursuit of utilitarian aims will sometimes be enhanced, but at the expense of justice to individuals. So the practice of punishment involves a compromise in which the pursuit of desirable general social aims is checked by the need to protect individuals from being used simply as a means to the fulfilment of these general social aims. Punishment is therefore distinguished from other measures for pursuing similar social aims, like the compulsory quarantine of people with infectious diseases in which the principles of justice do not apply.[22] Hart does not, however, claim that the constraints laid down by the principles of justice are absolute, and he entertains the possibility that in extreme situations, the innocent may have to be sacrificed. 'In extreme cases many might still think it right to resort to these expedients but we should do so with the sense of sacrificing an important principle. We should be conscious of choosing the lesser of two evils, and this would be inexplicable if the principle sacrificed to utility were itself only a requirement of utility.'[23]

Hart's theory resembles the Compromise Theory discussed

in the previous section. The Retributive Condition restricts the distribution of punishment in much the same way as Hart's principles of justice, and the Utilitarian Condition resembles Hart's claim that the General Justifying Aim of punishment is utilitarian. The difference between the two theories is that the Compromise Theory, unlike Hart's theory, does not break down the issues concerning the justification of punishment into separate questions about the General Justifying Aim and the Distribution of punishment. But this leads to a more important difference.

In Hart's theory, the promotion of utilitarian values as the General Justifying Aim can come into conflict with the principles of justice in Distribution, and if the constraint imposed by these principles will have catastrophic results, then the principles may have to be sacrificed. So in extreme situations the theory allows for the possibility of utilitarian considerations overriding the principles of justice, and the scope of punishment will then be extended to cover the punishment of those who have not voluntarily broken the law. On the other hand, the principles of justice could never require the punishment of the voluntary offender when no utilitarian value is thereby served since these principles are not part of the General Justifying Aim of punishment.

I agree with Hart that the practice of punishment could not be justified if it did not produce beneficial consequences. To that extent Hart is right in regarding the General Justifying Aim of punishment as utilitarian. But I have argued that once it is established that punishment, rather than some other social practice, is the preferred alternative for reducing crime, then retributive considerations can also provide positive reasons in support of punishment. This support may be crucial in situations in which the utilitarian case for punishment is insufficient, or even where there is a utilitarian case against punishment, though not of a particularly powerful kind. Thus the exception to the Utilitarian Condition permits the punishment of a serious offender in circumstances in which the strict utilitarian would consider the punishment to be unjustified.

The arguments leading up to the Revised Compromise Theory provide the basis for explaining why the practice of punishment takes the form that it does of generally confining punishment to those who have voluntarily violated legitimate laws. The constraint on the distribution of punishment is dictated by considerations which are internal to the practice of punishment, for that practice is shaped by a plurality of independent values, each with an irreducible role to play.

However, some critics of the practice of punishment believe that the criminal law is ill served by such a practice which is burdened by its recognition of legal excuses. They believe that the rational pursuit of the aim of crime prevention is better served by the adoption of a system of treatment in which legal excuses have no place. I now turn to a detailed examination of the rationale of legal excuses, and of the alleged superiority of a system of treatment.

TREATMENT WITHOUT THE EXCUSES OF
PUNISHMENT

5.1. *Hart's Rationale of Legal Excuses*

It is a characteristic feature of institutions of punishment that even when prohibited acts have been committed, offenders will not be punished if they successfully plead various excuses like duress, mistake, accident, and insanity. These excuses exempt from punishment a wider class of persons than those who are innocent of any legal offence. It is possible to have an alternative system of criminal law which dispenses with such excuses. Even in our own legal systems, there are specific 'strict liability' laws where, once the prohibited acts have been committed, offenders are not excused from punishment even though they did not intend to commit the acts, and had taken all reasonable precautions to avoid them. The selling of adulterated food is an example of a strict liability offence. The justification of strict liability offences is a matter of controversy to which I shall return later. But a system of criminal law which dispenses altogether with legal excuses would be one in which all offences, and not just a few here and there, are strict liability offences. Later in this chapter I shall examine one powerful and influential defence of such a system of criminal law, namely that presented by Lady Wootton. But first, it is important to see what we give up when we do away with legal excuses. A persuasive account of the rationale of legal excuses is given by H. L. A. Hart, and it is to his views again that I now turn.[1]

We have seen in the previous chapter that Hart defends what he calls 'the principles of justice' as governing the Distribution of punishment by confining punishment to those who have voluntarily broken the law. This is a constraint on the

---

[1] H. L. A. Hart, *Punishment and Responsibility* (Oxford, 1968), pp. 17–24, 28–53, 180–5, 206–9.

pursuit of the General Justifying Aim of punishment which is for Hart the utilitarian aim of preventing crime. Hart therefore rejects a purely utilitarian rationale of legal excuses. Such a rationale was offered by Jeremy Bentham. Bentham argued that punishment should not be inflicted when it is: (i) groundless in the sense that the act against which punishment was to be directed was harmless, or the harm done was outweighed by the good consequences of the act; (ii) inefficacious in that the punishment will not prevent any harm; (iii) unprofitable or too expensive when the harm inflicted by punishment is greater than the harm prevented by it; and (iv) needless where punishment is not the most economical way of preventing the harm done.[2]

Bentham believed that where a legal excuse was present, punishment would be inefficacious. When an offender had an excuse, punishment should not be inflicted because it would have no good effect on the conduct of the offender. For example, an infant could not be influenced by the threat of punishment. Nor could a person who was insane or intoxicated.[3]

But Hart argues against Bentham's view pointing out that while the threat of punishment would be ineffective against offenders who had an excuse, it does not follow that the punishment of these offenders would not reduce crime by deterring potential offenders, who might otherwise think that they could falsely but successfully plead one of the excuses.[4] Thus if insanity were an excuse, it might well be true, as Bentham claimed, that the threat of punishment would not be effective in preventing the genuinely insane person from engaging in criminal conduct. But at the same time the punishment of an insane offender might be effective in deterring normal offenders from committing crimes under the pretence that they were insane. The greater the number of excuses, the greater the opportunities for such deception. So from the purely utilitarian perspective, there are costs in recognizing excuses which have

---

[2] Jeremy Bentham, *An Introduction to the Principles of Morals and Legislation* (eds) J. H. Burns and H. L. A. Hart (London & New York, 1982), Ch. XIII.
[3] Ibid., p. 71.
[4] *Punishment and Responsibility*, p. 19. See also the persuasive objections to Bentham's theory given by George Fletcher, *Rethinking Criminal Law* (Boston & Toronto, 1978), pp. 813–17.

to be weighed against the benefits. Hart's argument does not rest on the claim that these costs are necessarily greater than the utilitarian benefits of recognizing excuses. The point is that the rationale of legal excuses lies elsewhere, and is not simply dependent on a utilitarian balancing of costs and benefits. It may be that when the utilitarian benefits of having a strict liability offence are sufficiently great, we are prepared to eliminate all excuses with respect to that offence. But even then, as Hart argues, we are conscious of having overridden an important principle.[5]

In a subtle and closely argued paper, T. L. S. Sprigge attempts to get round Hart's objections to Bentham's rationale of excuses.[6] Sprigge presents a new account of excuses which he claims is consistent with a broadly deterrent view of punishment. He maintains that punishment is the expression of blame, and when we blame someone we give 'a certain opinion of the state of will expressed in the conduct blamed, and this opinion carries with it a certain sentiment or feeling regarding the state of will'.[7] The essence of Sprigge's complex theory of moral responsibility is that we are justified in blaming someone when by so doing the following effects are produced: (i) the person blamed is made to acknowledge the truth of our opinion of his or her personality, and is thereby led to modify it in such a manner as to make the objectionable conduct less likely to recur; and (ii) our adverse opinion of the person blamed will help to modify or sustain our own dispositions and prevent us, and others like us, from developing the undesirable disposition which expressed itself in the conduct blamed.

Even when the first kind of effect is absent, blaming can still be justified in terms of the second kind of effect. For example, some selfish persons may be so settled in their selfishness that blaming them for their conduct will not affect them. But in such cases, those who do the blaming are aware that they themselves can easily become selfish unless they make the effort to avoid it. On the other hand, psychopaths are not to be blamed because blaming them will not produce

[5] Ibid., p. 20.
[6] T. L. S. Sprigge, 'Punishment and Moral Responsibility', in Milton Goldinger (ed.), *Punishment and Human Rights* (Cambridge, 1974), esp. pp. 88–96.
[7] Ibid., p. 90.

either type of effect. We do not therefore punish those offenders whose punishment will fail to produce either of the two effects mentioned. When offenders act under excusing conditions, their punishment will not have the desired effects.

Sprigge calls his theory 'the deterrent theory of moral responsibility'. The theory, unlike Bentham's, does not confine itself to the effects of punishment on the offender. Even so, it still ignores what for the utilitarian must be a very important effect that the punishment of the 'blameless', in Sprigge's sense, might have. For if Hart is right, then punishing 'blameless' offenders might have the desirable effect of reducing cases of simulated 'blameless' conduct. For example, even the punishment of psychopaths could be useful in deterring some normal people who would otherwise offend in the hope that, if caught, they would be excused by being mistaken for psychopathic offenders.

From the purely utilitarian point of view, if the effects are the same, it does not matter whether the crime rate is reduced by the fear of the unpleasantness of punishment, or because punishment engages people's conscientious feelings. Both the effects of blaming that Sprigge mentions are of the latter kind. However, apart from the persons blamed and those who participate in blaming them, there is a third class of persons whose moral feelings are not affected by blame, but whose conduct is none the less affected by the fear of the unpleasantness of being blamed. Blaming, as the passing of adverse moral judgement with its attendant sentiments, is itself an act which, from the utilitarian point of view, must be justified solely in terms of its consequences. So there is point in blaming if the third class of persons are favourably affected, even if blaming has neither of the effects specified by Sprigge.

Of course, if, as Sprigge rightly suggests, punishment is the expression of blame, it would be odd for the judge, in passing a sentence on an offender, to say, 'I do not blame you for what you have done, but a spell in prison (or whatever) may discourage you and others from acting thus again'.[8] This is odd because, on the one hand, the judge is acknowledging that the offender is blameless, while, on the other hand, he is being sent to prison as a form of punishment (which is an expression of blame). Up to this point Sprigge is right. But when punishing or blaming will not have the two types of effects that Sprigge mentions, a utilitarian judge is much more likely to say to the offender: 'Punishing you by putting you in prison (or whatever) will discourage others from acting as you did, and that is why we punish (or blame) you.' If there is still something odd in this remark, then its oddity is not conceptual but moral. It is unfair to blame an offender under these circumstances, but Sprigge has not shown that it is part of the concept of blaming, part of what we mean by *blaming*, that blaming is an act which engages people's conscientious feelings in the manner suggested.

Hart himself defends legal excuses on three main grounds: (i) their recognition maximizes individual liberty; (ii) they are required by justice to individuals which sets fair terms only on the basis of which may the claims of the rest of society be met; (iii) they reflect important distinctions which pervade the whole of our life in a society of persons.

(i) The recognition of excuses increases both our powers of predicting and of controlling when the law will interfere with our lives. For example, I am able to predict with a great deal of confidence whether I shall intentionally engage in harmful conduct, but not whether I shall accidentally do so. I have control over my intentional acts in the way that I lack similar control over my accidental acts. If therefore I may be punished even for accidental wrongdoing, then I shall not be able to foresee when I shall be punished, and I shall lack control over whether or when I shall fall foul of the law. My choices will not be effective in determining whether the law will interfere with my life, for when I cause harm accidentally, it is not through my choice that the harm eventuates. On the other hand, when I am punished for intentional acts, what happens to me results from a choice that I have made to act in certain ways. By not punishing me whenever I have an excuse, the law makes my choices effective in determining the future course of my life. And if I should choose to break the law and as a result punishment is inflicted on me, then I shall at least gain the satisfaction that punishment is the price I paid for a deliberate violation of the law.[9]

[9] *Punishment and Responsibility*, p. 47.

Hart further argues that the value of legal excuses is un-affected by the truth of any doctrine or determinism which maintains that all our actions are causally determined. Even if it could be shown that my choices are the products of a set of sufficient conditions of which I have no knowledge, this does not remove the satisfaction I get both from the exercise of choice and from the knowledge that it was my choice which on a particular occasion affected the outcome of events.[10]

Some of Hart's critics have pointed out that the gains that Hart thinks are produced by the law's recognition of excuses will have to be weighed against similar losses.[11] Hart suggests that the elimination of legal excuses might increase the general deterrent effect of punishment, and thereby reduce crime. The critics argue that such a reduction in crime will also enlarge the individual's freedom. Crime interferes with the lives of its victims, and thereby decreases the effectiveness of their own choices in determining the course of their lives. So a balancing of the losses and gains of having legal excuses, as opposed to strict liability offences, can be made, and it is suggested that sometimes at least the balance will go against the recognition of legal excuses. One critic, Gertrude Ezorsky, distinguishes between total strict liability, in which all offences are strict liability offences, and specific strict liability when offenders against only some laws are held strictly liable.[12] She suggests that whereas the utilitarian argument against total strict liability is overwhelming, the utilitarian case for specific strict liability offences will sometimes be just as decisive.

Hart's argument is particularly powerful against a system of total strict liability. But of course he would not deny that with respect to a specific offence, the utilitarian case for strict liability may be decisive. He also acknowledges that a particular excuse like insanity or mental abnormality may be eliminated.[13] More generally, he points out that the law's

[10] Ibid., p. 46. The issue of free will, determinism, and moral responsibility is long standing and contentious. For a recent discussion, see Daniel C. Dennett, *Elbow Room* (Oxford, 1984). In *Philosophical Explanations* (Oxford, 1981), pp. 393–7, Robert Nozick argues that determinism is irrelevant to his version of retributive punishment. I discuss Nozick's retributivism in Ch. 3.

[11] Gertrude Ezorsky, 'Punishment and Excuses', in Milton Goldinger (ed.), *Punishment and Human Rights*, pp. 106–7; and Ronald Dworkin, *Taking Rights Seriously* (London, 1978), p. 10.   [12] 'Punishment and Excuses', p. 104.

[13] *Punishment and Responsibility*, p. 205.

recognition of excuses can sometimes be applied in 'dangerous ways'.[14] For example, in 1961 a man, who was tried for the murder of a woman, successfully pleaded that he had killed her in his sleep, and was accordingly acquitted and discharged altogether. So Hart is well aware of the utilitarian costs of legal excuses, but he believes that the values embodied in the recognition of legal excuses act as distributive constraints on the pursuit of purely utilitarian aims, and cannot therefore derive their significance simply from their contribution to those aims. If he is right here, then the value of legal excuses cannot simply lie in their beneficial consequences in increasing individual freedom, for that can sometimes be outweighed, as the critics suggest, by other similar beneficial consequences that the reduction of crime might bring. The value of legal excuses must in the end rest on the protection that it extends to individuals of not being used in certain ways for the benefit of society. There is a link to be made shortly between Hart's first and second arguments for legal excuses.

But Hart is also concerned to show that the increase in freedom is one of the values promoted by the acknowledgement of legal excuses. His argument pinpoints the price we may have to pay for maximizing individual freedom. For if indeed the removal of legal excuses reduces crime, then the main benefits of such reduction may lie not so much in the increase in individual freedom, but in the avoidance of harms like physical and mental suffering, and the loss of material goods. But it remains true that an increase in crime as a result of recognizing legal excuses will also reduce at least to some extent the freedom of individuals, just as legal excuses enlarge individual liberty in the manner suggested by Hart. So has Hart simply overlooked the fact that even with respect to the single value of individual freedom, the acceptance of legal excuses both increases individual freedom in one direction and cuts it back in another?

The answer is that the freedom lost as a result of the failure to acknowledge legal excuses is particularly repugnant because it is compounded by the condemnation through punishment of conduct which one could not reasonably have avoided. (In a system of total strict liability, it is conceivable that

[14] Ibid., p. 201.

punishment, and with it the condemnation of offenders or the expressions of blame directed at them, will be replaced by treatment in which no one is blamed at all. I shall discuss this later. But we are now dealing with specific strict liability.) On the other hand, the victims of crime are not subjected to similar condemnation, for it is the criminal's interference with his victim's plans, and not the victim's action, which is regarded as socially undesirable. Now this difference is important not merely because it means that, other things being equal, there is an additional harm that is inflicted on strict liability offenders, but also because the nature of this harm is such that it raises distinctly distributive issues. For so long as it is a matter of weighing the welfare and liberty of two perhaps partially overlapping groups, on the one hand the new victims of crime, and on the other hand, the morally innocent strict liability offenders, a utilitarian balancing of their respective interests would be appropriate. No one group can claim that its interests count for more than the similar interests of the other group. Both groups share the risks that their welfare and freedom will be interfered with through no choice of their own. But strict liability offences introduce the element of unfairness to some individuals by punishing them as a direct means to the promotion of the welfare and freedom of others. When we develop Hart's first argument in this way, it merges into his second argument for legal excuses.

(ii) Hart points out that legal excuses serve to protect individuals from the excessive claims of the rest of society by ensuring that the terms on which such claims may be made are fair. These terms can only be fair if they give effect to the individual's choices. Society needs what Hart calls a 'moral licence' to punish. The terms of this licence are that individuals should have the capacity and fair opportunity to conform to the law. It is only then that they are not used as mere instruments for the promotion of society's goals, for it is only then that their own choices will determine whether they are liable to punishment. Thus mental illness may deprive people of the capacity to obey the law. Again, if people are unable to understand the demands of the law or, having understood them, are unable to act in accordance with those demands even when they try to, then they lack the necessary capacity. On the other hand, people may have the normal capacities to conform to the law, but may lack fair opportunity to obey the law. Thus they lack such opportunity to obey the law if they are liable to punishment even when they have taken all reasonable precautions to avoid violating the law, or when they are under duress to break the law.

Hart argues for legal excuses as constraints on the pursuit of desirable social aims. But he does not suggest that, so long as we observe these constraints and give effect to people's choices, then our treatment of others is automatically justified no matter what our aims may be. Hence the objections of one recent critic are completely off the mark. Richard W. Burgh argues that if a group of terrorists gave their hostages a fair opportunity to escape being beaten by making it plain to them that those who attempt to escape would be beaten, this would not make the beating just. Nor is the beating just if the terrorists further informed the hostages that they would receive positive benefits if they did as they were told.[15] What is absent from Burgh's account is any justification of the activities of the terrorists in taking innocent people as hostages, and in the absence of that, the activities of the terrorists are very different from the practice of punishing offenders which is for the benefit of the community. Burgh's mistake is to treat the giving of fair opportunities as in itself a sufficient condition of justice in our treatment of others.

Although a system of excuses operates against the background where punishment is generally directed to the reduction of crime, it is now obvious that Hart's rationale of excuses is neither utilitarian nor is it always compatible with a purely utilitarian rationale. A just distribution of punishment, which confines punishment to those without excuses, may have the effect of reducing the efficacy of the law in preventing crime. The utilitarian aim of maximizing happiness, or maximizing the satisfaction of desires, without regard to the way in which these desirable states are distributed, may be hampered to some extent by the adoption of Hart's moral licence. We have now to ask how Hart's rationale of legal excuses stands in relation to the retributive theory.

The terms of the moral licence imposed on society by the recognition of legal excuses may be the same as those on which the retributivist would insist. But Hart argues that the purpose of the licence is to prevent future crimes and not, as the retributivist maintains, to punish moral wrongdoing, or to pay back the harm that offenders have done.[16] Whereas Hart's rationale of legal excuses is independent of the Utilitarianism which he accepts as the General Justifying Aim of punishment, retributivists base their account of excuses on the theory of Retribution as the General Justifying Aim. But it is possible to bring the two accounts closer together.

The retributivist confines punishment to those who deserve it. This obviously rules out the punishment of those who have not committed any offence. But in order to have a rationale of excuses, those to be exempted from punishment must include some offenders. These are offenders who do not deserve punishment, and are not blameworthy even though their acts are wrong. For an excuse is different from a justification even though in both cases there is no liability to punishment. A person who kills in order to defend his life has a legal (and moral) justification in the sense that killing in self-defence is not considered wrong. On the other hand, when a person is excused for accidental killing, the act itself is still regarded as wrong or deplorable, but the agent is absolved from responsibility for it.[17]

Nozick provides a general framework for explaining excuses within a retributive theory. He writes: 'The punishment

[15] Richard W. Burgh, 'Do the Guilty Deserve Punishment?', *The Journal of Philosophy*, 79 (1982), pp. 198–201.   [16] *Punishment and Responsibility*, pp. 201, 208.

[17] Ibid., pp. 13–4. See also J. L. Austin, 'A Plea for Excuses', in J. L. Austin, *Philosophical Papers* (eds) J. O. Urmson and G. J. Warnock (Oxford, 1961), pp. 123–5. An interesting elaboration of the distinction between a justification and an excuse is given by George Fletcher in *Rethinking Criminal Law*, pp. 810–13. Fletcher argues that a justification provides a precedent that can be applied to future similar cases whereas excuses do not create such precedents. Indeed he goes further to suggest that 'precedents have an inverse effect on the excusability of similar conduct in the future' (p. 812). He cites a case of an acquittal of a prisoner who escaped from jail in order to avoid a homosexual rape. If another prisoner's decision to escape relied on this case as precedent, then he might be convicted because it would appear that his escape was set off more by the prospect of legal immunity than by the threat of rape. On the other hand, if there had been a series of convictions for those who escape from prison in order to avoid rape, then a prisoner who made a subsequent escape in the knowledge of these convictions could have an excuse because he acted out of desperation and fear. However, Fletcher's argument fails to show that the excuse does not set up a precedent for all similar cases. The cases cited are not similar precisely because they differ with respect to motivations.

deserved depends on the magnitude H of the wrongness of the act, and the person's degree of responsibility r for the act, and is equal in magnitude to their product, $r \times H$.'[18] The degree of responsibility varies from full responsibility, when r has the value of 1, to no responsibility when $r = 0$. Nozick suggests that excuses lower r while justifications lower H.[19] This is a useful formal framework indicating that in order to show that an offender has an excuse, and therefore does not deserve punishment, the retributivist would need to argue that he had no responsibility for his act.

To this formal account, Nozick adds a more substantive account according to which excuses show that an act of wrong-doing did not stem from a defect of character.[20] Offenders are only punished for those acts of theirs which are expressions of defects of character.

George Fletcher, who also connects legal excuses with the absence of character defects, argues that in the presence of an excusing condition we cannot make an inference, which is otherwise permissible, from the act to the agent's character.[21] For example, we can normally infer that a bank teller who gives money to a stranger is dishonest. But if he gives the money at gunpoint, then we cannot infer anything about his honesty. Fletcher acknowledges the limitation of inferring an offender's character from just a single wrongful act, but accepts this as the price we have to pay in order to protect his or her privacy. However, it has been argued by Michael D. Bayles that in making an inference about the offender's character, we do not just rely on his behaviour but also on his mental state which indicates his attitude.[22] A dangerous act of discharging a gun in a crowded room is evidence of an undesirable charac-ter when it is done purposely, knowingly, or recklessly, but not when it is done accidentally. Thus a person who purposely

---

[18] *Philosophical Explanations,*p. 363.

[19] Ibid., p. 719 n. 82.

[20] Ibid., p. 383.

[21] *Rethinking Criminal Law*, pp. 799–802. But Fletcher points out that the theory seems to rest on the implausible assumption that people choose to develop the charac-ter they have (p. 805). He is also quite enthusiastic about Hart's rationale of excuses.

[22] Michael D. Bayles, 'Character, Purpose, and Criminal Responsibility', *Law and Philosophy*, 1(1982), p. 10. Bayles gives a lucid defence of the theory without however connecting it with retributivism. He believes that blameworthiness is not a sufficient but only a necessary condition for justifiable punishment (p. 8).

causes harm displays an undesirable attitude towards such harm in that he wants the harm to occur. Bayles goes on to suggest that, 'While attitudes may be fleeting, the law uses a general presumption that the combination of behaviour and attitude indicates an undesirable character trait, and excuses are designed to show that the normal inference is not warranted.'[23] This is illuminating, but it does not entirely account for the crucial importance that the law attaches to the particular attitude displayed in an act of wrongdoing, even when this attitude may be out of character. An honest bank teller may act dishonestly on a specific occasion without having an excuse. We cannot infer that he has a dishonest disposition, but his act is still punishable, although perhaps the punishment should be mitigated. When however we are dealing with persistent offenders who lack excuses, then the inference to character from a series of acts is better based, and that may be a reason why, from the retributive point of view, such offenders deserve more severe punishment.

It would perhaps be more appropriate to claim that excuses show that the offending act is not the expression of an undesirable moral attitude, irrespective of whether this attitude is part of a settled disposition. Conversely, intentional wrongdoing is the expression of a morally undesirable attitude, even if it is out of character. Nozick comes close to this position when he maintains that, 'The excuse does not show that the agent does not have a defect of character, even one that could lead to this act, but it shows that this act did not stem from that defect of character.'[24]

A theory of excuses in terms of the role of excuses in denying character defects is different from Hart's theory, but generally the two theories do not appear to be incompatible. On Hart's view, it would be unfair to punish a person for the benefit of society unless he had the capacity and opportunity to avoid such punishment. A retributivist would say that no person should be punished unless he is morally culpable or blameworthy for his conduct. The two views yield the same excuses if the conditions under which a person lacks the capacity or

---

[23] Ibid., p. 10.

[24] *Philosophical Explanations*, p. 383. Nozick seems to use the notion of excuses in a broad sense to cover mitigation as well.

fair opportunity to obey the law are the same as those which make him blameless for his conduct, and they seem to be the same.

The account of excuses that forms part of Herbert Morris's retributive theory links excuses with distributive considerations in a manner that is in some respects strikingly similar to Hart's theory. It will be recalled that, according to Morris, punishment is justified in terms of its restoration of the equilibrium of benefits and burdens. He explicitly argues that provision must be made within the system of punishment to ensure that the system does not itself promote an unfair distribution of benefits and burdens. Only offenders who have derived unfair advantages for themselves should be punished. 'A person has not derived an unfair advantage if he could not have restrained himself or if it is unreasonable to expect him to behave otherwise than he did.'[25] To punish those who have not voluntarily renounced a burden that others have assumed is itself to cause an unfair distribution of benefits and burdens. Morris connects punishment to 'a freely chosen act violative of the rules', and his system of punishment seeks to minimize 'the chances of punishment of those who have not chosen to do acts violative of the rules'.[26] So he too links legal excuses with the importance attached to the choices of individuals, and draws a connection between the exercise of individual choices and the gaining of unfair advantages over others.

(iii) Hart's third argument for legal excuses is based on certain very deep and pervasive features of social life. 'Human society' Hart writes, 'is a society of persons', and 'persons interpret each other's movements as manifestations of intention and choices, and these subjective factors are more important to their social relations than the movements by which they are manifested or their effects.'[27] People respond very differently to harm caused by others, depending on their judgements about whether the harm was deliberately inflicted or accidental. 'This is how human nature in human society actually is and as yet we have no power to alter it.'[28] It is

[25] Herbert Morris, 'Persons and Punishment', in Jeffrie G. Murphy (ed.), *Punishment and Rehabilitation*, p. 43.
[26] Ibid., p. 50.
[27] *Punishment and Responsibility*, p. 182.
[28] Ibid., p. 183.

important therefore that the law should reflect those distinctions which pervade our social life and which we find it impossible to remove, even if we wanted to.

There are several ways of developing this argument. First, suppose that the law, by not recognizing excuses, fails to reflect the distinction that is of vast importance in the rest of social life between deliberately causing harm and causing harm accidentally. It can be argued that the law will differ so radically from the rest of social life that the law cannot function effectively. People will not understand why someone who has caused harm accidentally would be liable to punishment, and in cases where it was obvious that the harm was indeed accidental, juries will refuse to convict. The law will increasingly lose the respect of the community for whom it was supposed to benefit. But even if the law is faithfully applied, there will be certain undesirable consequences of its application. Just because the law refuses to make the distinctions which are vital in our social relations, it does not follow that those distinctions will cease to be important, or be ignored when evaluations are made of the offender. So, for example, suppose that a man causes the death of his wife. He will be convicted, and will be liable to punishment independently of whether he killed deliberately or accidentally. But both his and his wife's families and their friends would be interested to know whether there was an excuse, for that would be crucial in determining their attitudes and the future course of their relations to him. If the law regards the issue as irrelevant and there is no public inquiry into it, the issue will still be pursued by innuendoes and gossips. It will not be laid to rest simply because the law ignores it.

Dworkin puts a different gloss on Hart's argument when he suggests that the argument urges that 'the government must treat its citizens with the respect and dignity that adult members of the community claim from each other'.[29] People make a distinction between acts which they feel that they have chosen and over which they have control, and acts which are the product of accident, compulsion, duress, or disease. This distinction is important not only in their judgements of their own

---

[29] *Taking Rights Seriously*, p. 11.

conduct, but also in their attitudes towards others. If the government is to show respect to its citizens, it must take account of this distinction, and view their conduct from the same perspective. This interpretation of Hart's third argument, by stressing the importance of individual choice, links it to the second argument discussed earlier. Central to Hart's case for legal excuses is the view that where such excuses are present, offenders do not have control over their actions. On the other hand, where excuses are absent, offenders act in accordance with their own choices and in the light of their own values, attitudes, and beliefs. The recognition of excuses promotes the autonomy of individuals in guiding their conduct in accordance with their own conceptions of how their lives should be run.

It is now important to consider whether those who unintentionally but negligently cause harm should be excused. Is it fair to punish such negligent conduct, and if so, is there a moral basis for distinguishing between criminal negligence and strict liability offences?

5.2. Mens Rea, *Negligence, and Strict Liability*

The law uses the term *mens rea* (a guilty mind) to refer to those mental elements of conduct which are necessary for criminal conviction and punishment. For example, intentional killing is killing with *mens rea*, whereas *mens rea* is absent in accidentally causing death. To act with *mens rea* is to act without a legal excuse. In giving a rationale of legal excuses Hart has therefore also given a general defence of the doctrine of *mens rea* against crimes of strict liability or absolute liability in which the requirement of *mens rea* for criminal liability is dropped.[30] But the scope of the doctrine of *mens rea* is controversial. There is

---

[30] It has been pointed out that offences which are called strict liability offences do not really involve absolute liability in the sense that no excuses at all are recognized. Such absolute liability offences are very rare. See Hyman Gross, *A Theory of Criminal Justice* (New York, 1979), p. 343, and T. Brian Hogan, *Criminal Liability Without Fault*, An Inaugural Lecture (Cambridge, 1969), p. 7. I have however used the terms 'strict' and 'absolute' liability interchangeably. Many of those who condemn or defend strict liability offences focus on the fact that offenders are not culpable for they could not reasonably have avoided committing the offence. In such cases, whether or not the strict liability offences would have allowed for *some* excuses, the fact remains that the only excuses which are relevant or available, and which would have been accepted in other cases, are not recognized. Where an offence, which is *called* a strict liability offence, in fact requires at least negligence to be shown, it is not the type of offence that I have in mind when I refer to strict liability.

dispute over whether a person who causes harm negligently acted with or without *mens rea*. It is sometimes claimed that to make persons criminally liable for causing harm negligently is to make this into a strict liability offence. Before assessing this claim we need to know what is involved in acting negligently.

Let us begin by distinguishing between recklessness and negligence. When a person causes harm recklessly, he or she does not intend to cause the harm, but foresees that the course of action taken runs a significant or substantial risk of causing harm, and chooses to proceed with the action without a social justification, and without taking reasonable precautions to avoid the harm. On the other hand, when someone causes harm negligently, he or she does not intend to cause the harm, is unaware that the action runs the risk of causing harm, but the harm results from a failure to observe a reasonable standard of care. In both recklessness and negligence there is failure to observe certain standards of care. We expect people to take precautions when they engage in activities which run the risk of causing harm to others. The standards of care required are those which a reasonable person would have taken in the circumstances. But in the case of recklessness, a subjective element is also present in that the reckless person foresees the risk of harm. Is it the case that in negligence we employ a purely objective test of what the reasonable person would have done without any reference to the agent's subjective state?

Hart agrees that negligence does not involve a subjective mental element if by this we mean that the offender should have had the intention to cause the harm, or that he at least foresaw the possibility of the harm eventuating. But he points out that from this it does not follow that 'mere inadvertence' is sufficient for negligent conduct. For example, suppose that a negligent workman, repairing a roof in a busy town, throws down slates to the street below. He did not foresee that he would harm others by his action, but at the same time it is not satisfactory to say that he merely acted in a fit of inadvertence. In calling his act negligent, we are also blaming him for failure to take the sort of precautions to avoid harm to others which a reasonable person would have taken. Because negligence refers to the failure to comply with certain standards of care, it can admit of degrees. The workman was grossly negligent if he did not even look down to see that the street was empty before throwing off the slates, and less negligent if he did not shout a warning for those not yet in view.[31] So unlike inadvertence, which refers to the absence of foresight of consequences and thus does not admit of degrees, there can be degrees of negligence depending on the stringency of the standards with which the negligent person failed to comply. Those guilty of gross negligence have failed to satisfy very low standards; they have failed to take very elementary precautions against harming others.

Hart goes on to distinguish between two questions which should be used to test for criminal negligence:

(i) Did the accused fail to take those precautions which any reasonable man with normal capacities would in the circumstances have taken?

(ii) Could the accused, given his mental and physical capacities, have taken those precautions?[32]

The first question relies on a standard which is often called 'objective', while the second embodies a 'subjective' standard or test. But Hart prefers to refer to them as an 'invariant standard of care' and 'individualised conditions of liability' respectively. On Hart's view, the tests for negligence should include not just the first, but also the second, question, because these tests should be adjusted to the mental and physical capacities of the accused. In making this adjustment, we satisfy the general conditions which, as we have seen in the previous section, Hart lays down for an offender to be excused from punishment, namely that he lacks either the capacity or the fair opportunity to comply with the requirements of the law.[33]

[31] *Punishment and Responsibility*, p. 149.

[32] Ibid., p. 154. But see also p. 261 where Hart adds some important qualifications.

[33] Wasserstrom maintains that it is only in the case of deliberate, intentional conduct, but not in the case of negligent conduct, that the agent chose to break the law. He argues that Hart's defence of the doctrine of *mens rea*, which stresses the value of such choices, does not therefore apply to negligent conduct. See Richard A. Wasserstrom, 'H. L. A. Hart and the Doctrines of *Mens Rea* and Criminal Responsibility', *The University of Chicago Law Review*, 35 (1967), pp. 103–4. However, Wasserstrom overlooks the point that ultimately for Hart criminal responsibility is present only when offenders have the capacity and fair opportunity to obey the law, and while intentional conduct is sufficient to establish the presence of this capacity and opportunity, it is not necessary.

If the accused caused harm to others, and applying the two questions to him will yield affirmative answers, then we know that he had both the capacity and opportunity to take those precautions which a reasonable person would have taken, but which the accused omitted to take.

In an otherwise most valuable article, M. T. Thornton takes Hart to task for calling the second question 'subjective'.[34] Thornton complains: 'It would simply be a play on words to assert that a subjectivist about negligence (one who favours a variable standard) is a subjectivist about *mens rea* (one who requires a requirement of intention, knowledge or recklessness).'[35] But of course Hart makes no such claim, and indeed, as we have just seen, even warns against the use of the confusing terms 'subjective' and 'objective'. Hart's substantial point is that holding people criminally responsible for negligent acts is only morally defensible and morally distinguishable from strict liability if the test for negligence is adjusted to the capacities of the accused. On this issue, Thornton seems to agree at least up to a point, for he too cites the use of a variable standard in negligence as a feature which distinguishes criminal negligence from strict liability. But he goes on to argue that negligence is distinguishable from strict liability whether or not the variable standard for negligence is applied. His argument here rests on the claim that someone who commits a strict liability offence is not acting unreasonably because he is blamelessly inadvertent. He is blamelessly inadvertent in the sense that even a reasonable person would in the circumstances also have committed a similar act. This establishes a difference between strict liability and negligence because in the case of negligence, a person who acted as a reasonable person would have done, would not be liable to punishment. But is the difference morally significant if the variable standard is abandoned? A person could then be criminally negligent because he failed to act as the reasonable person would have done even though he did not have the capacity of the reasonable person. Is it fair to punish someone when he had taken all the reasonable precautions that *he* could have taken?

[34] M. T. Thornton, 'Rape and Mens Rea', in Kai Nielsen and Steven C. Patten (eds), *New Essays in Ethics and Public Policy, Canadian Journal of Philosophy*, Supplementary Vol. 8 (1982), pp. 123–4.   [35] Ibid., pp. 123–4.

The point here can be strengthened by a consideration of
the moral justification for punishing negligent rape, which is
the broader context of Thornton's discussion. He refers to the
controversial *Morgan* rape case. Morgan invited three of his
colleagues home to have sexual intercourse with his wife, telling
them that she would welcome intercourse even though she
might simulate resistance. The men forcibly had sexual intercourse with Mrs Morgan who put up a fierce resistance. They
were convicted. The point of law as to whether the defendant
to a rape charge could be properly convicted if he believed
that the woman was consenting, even though the belief was
not based on reasonable grounds, was referred to the House
of Lords. In 1975 the law lords unanimously upheld the convictions, but decided by a 3–2 majority that a defendant could
not be found guilty of rape if in fact he believed that the woman
consented, whether or not the belief was based on reasonable
grounds. I shall not be concerned here with the actual legal
situation in any particular country, but rather with the moral
issue about what the law ought to be in this type of case.

In the case of rape, the prohibited act is having sexual
intercourse with a woman without her consent. The moral
issue then is what the requirements of *mens rea* should be if
the offender is to be fairly punished for committing the prohibited act. Thornton states the requirement of 'subjective' *mens
rea* as follows: '. . . unless the agent either intended the intercourse to be without the woman's consent or knew that she
did not consent or was reckless as to whether or not she consented, he cannot be guilty of rape'.[36] On the other hand,
those, like Thornton himself, who believe that 'objective' *mens
rea* is sufficient, argue that a man is still guilty of rape if he
had sexual intercourse with a woman without her consent and
unreasonably believed that she was consenting. The effect of
accepting 'objective' *mens rea* is that a person can be guilty
of rape through negligence.

Thornton mounts a persuasive case for the offence of negligent rape.[37] He argues that when an agent's mistaken belief

[36] Ibid., p. 124.
[37] Ibid., pp. 132–7. It has also been argued that a defendant to a rape charge who
believed that the woman consented could still have acted recklessly. See: E. M.
Curley, 'Excusing Rape', *Philosophy and Public Affairs*, 5 (1976); Anthony Kenny,

that his victim was consenting is not based on reasonable grounds, then he manifests lack of respect for the victim, and uses her simply as a means to his own pleasure. Thus he owes it to the victim to take her struggle seriously as evidence of lack of consent, and not to accept as decisive the assurance of a third party that the resistance is only simulated. The failure to do so suggests that the agent was not very concerned about the victim's welfare and point of view.

The argument is convincing, but only because there is an implicit assumption that the person guilty of negligent rape had normal capacities. For suppose instead that we have independent evidence that his capacities were so defective that he could not distinguish between the victim's resistance and her consent, or understand the significance of her resistance. If an invariant standard for negligence were applied, then the agent would be found guilty of rape. But now there is no basis for claiming that his conduct displayed a lack of respect for his victim, or that he treated her simply as a means to his own pleasure. Thus the moral case for making negligent rape a criminal offence does seem to rest on the application of a variable standard of reasonableness. Thornton admits as much when he refuses to accept rape as a strict liability offence: 'One does not have to be a retributivist about culpability to feel that a defendant must have had a fair opportunity to conform to the law's requirements and that if he hasn't then it is unfair to hold him criminally or morally responsible.'[38] This of course echoes Hart's view.

The case for including negligence in *mens rea* shows that it is fair to make people criminally liable for their negligent conduct. But can we go further and maintain that even punishment for strict liability offences is fair? It is of course one thing to argue that strict liability offences, though they are unfair because they allow the punishment of blameless offenders, is none the less justified because the unfairness is outweighed by other values, namely the good consequences produced by, for example, the simplification of the law and the ease of getting convictions. But it is quite another thing to maintain that such

Freewill and Responsibility (London, 1978), Ch. 3. Thornton rejects their views on pp. 126–8.

[38] 'Rape and Mens Rea', p. 137.

offences are fair. It is only this latter point that I shall now discuss, for it is the notion of fairness which is relevant to whether there is a legitimate excuse.

In a well-known paper, Richard A. Wasserstrom argues for the greater deterrent effect of strict liability offences, but he also maintains that strict liability offenders can be said to be at fault.[39] He cites the case of *State* v. *Lindberg* (1923) in which the defendant was convicted for violation of a statute which stated that 'every director and officer of any bank . . . who shall borrow . . . any of its funds in an excessive amount . . . shall . . . be guilty of a felony'.[40] Although the defendant claimed that he had borrowed the money only after being assured by another bank official that the loan was not from his own bank, the court held that the reasonableness of the mistake was no defence. Wasserstrom comments: '. . . there was a conscious intent to engage in just that activity—banking—which the defendant knew and should have known to be subject to criminal sanctions under certain specified circumstances'.[41] On Wasserstrom's view a person can be at fault even though his conduct was non-negligent.

Gertrude Ezorsky suggests illuminatingly that Wasserstrom's position is that the following condition, which she calls *risk*, is sufficient to establish the presence of fault for involuntary offences:

> B is a legally prohibited act. The agent knows that, if in doing A voluntarily he does B involuntarily, his excuse for doing B would not be accepted as a defence against criminal sanctions.

The agent in doing A voluntarily does B involuntarily.[42] Ezorsky goes on to deny that *risk* is sufficient to establish fault. She illustrates her point with an example of a druggist who is convicted of the strict liability offence of selling, without a written order, a substance containing narcotics. He has carefully taken all reasonable precautions, but a competitor had

[39] Richard A. Wasserstrom, 'Strict Liability in the Criminal Law', *Stanford Law Review*, 12 (1959–60).

[40] Quoted by Wasserstrom, ibid., p. 733.

[41] Ibid., p. 743.

[42] Gertrude Ezorsky, 'Punishment and Excuses', p. 100.

substituted indistinguishable bottles of syrup spiked with narcotics for bottles of cough syrup. Although *risk* obtains, the
druggist cannot be said to be at fault. One could imagine a
banker facing a similar situation in which his colleagues have
conspired to misinform him about the origins of his loan. No
matter how many times or how extensively he checked, they
had arranged that he would get the same false information.

But Wasserstrom would presumably reply that no one has
to be a druggist or a banker, and no one who voluntarily
becomes a banker needs to take a loan; and any one who
enters an occupation knowing that strict liability rules apply
there, is at fault if he or she falls foul of these rules. Now the
strength of this reply depends on the ease or difficulty with
which one can avoid a particular occupation or activity where
strict liability rules apply. So the argument is inapplicable to
a system of total strict liability which leaves no room for escape
from the operation of these rules. Secondly, the argument will
also not support strict liability offences in areas where one
could cause harm to others simply in the normal course of
social life. For example, killing and injuring others cannot in
general be strict liability offences, although killing and injuring
with a strange and rarely used weapon may be. It looks as if
Wasserstrom himself will accept the limited scope of his argument, for he writes: 'Strict liability offences can be interpreted
as legislative judgments that persons who intentionally engage
in certain activities and *occupy some peculiar or distinctive position*
of control are to be held accountable for the occurrence of
certain consequences.'[43]

Finally, we must ask whether Wasserstrom's argument carries much weight even when applied to activities which one
can easily avoid. Here it must be remembered that the relevant
activities are perfectly legitimate, and some of them are socially
very desirable. One could perhaps agree that an offender is
at fault if at the time of deciding to engage in the activity, he
knows that he is likely to violate the law, or if he has good
reason to believe that his personal qualities are such that he
is more likely than the average person to breach the law. He
can also be said to be at fault if he does not quit the activity,

[43] 'Strict Liability in the Criminal Law', p. 743. The emphasis is mine.

assuming that this is possible, if he subsequently acquires the relevant knowledge or belief about his inability to conform to the requirements of the law. But where such knowledge or belief is unavailable, there is no reason why he should not participate in the activity. The fact that he could have avoided the activity does not render him at fault for violation of the strict liability rules governing it, for he has no reason to believe that he, rather than someone else, will violate the rules.

Ezorsky thinks that there are circumstances in which the punishment of blameless offenders, as a result of the application of strict liability rules, would be justified. The punishment is justified when it involves a type of sacrifice which she thinks that we have a duty to make. A person A has a duty of sacrifice to members of a B group when 'There is a very great gap between the distress A would suffer because of his sacrifice and the greater degree of distress B would be spared thereby.'[44] Thus even though A is blameless and his punishment is undeserved, the punishment is justified if A's distress were *very much* less than the harm which potential victims of crime are spared because of his punishment. Ezorsky's requirement for there to be a duty of A to B is clear enough when A and B are two individuals. But sometimes, as in the case of A's punishment for the benefit of others, the benficiaries are a group of persons. I shall assume that in these cases Ezorsky would not support the sacrifice of A even when the aggregate of the distress of the B group is much greater than A's distress, but would insist further that the distress of at least one member of the group is much greater than A's.

In her discussion of strict liability, Ezorsky wishes to confine the justified punishment of blameless offenders to those whose punishment would satisfy two further conditions: (i) their punishment would not deceive the community into believing that they were at fault (no deception condition); (ii) the offences for which they are to be punished are those in which the *risk* condition, as defined earlier, holds.[45]

The no deception condition is needed to remove the source of an additional complaint which blameless offenders who are punished would have if their punishment made the community

---

[44] 'Punishment and Excuses', p. 110.
[45] Ibid., pp. 102–3.

falsely believe that they were blameworthy. The *risk* condition is imposed so that blameless offenders will not be the victims of the unfairness of failing to receive due notice. Those who fail to receive such notice are unable to make adjustments to their activities. When these two conditions are satisfied, Ezorsky argues that the punishment of a blameless offender is justified if it prevented much greater undeserved suffering to another person who would otherwise be the victim of crime.

I assume that Ezorsky's argument is intended to show that, under the circumstances described, strict liability is justified even though it involves the unfairness of punishing blameless offenders. Put in those terms, her argument can be accepted, and it does not affect the case against the fairness of strict liability offences. It is obvious, for example, that the satisfaction of the *risk* condition, although it removes one kind of unfairness, is insufficient to ensure fairness in the treatment of the offender. A bank robber can give due notice to the cashiers that he will shoot them unless they hand over the money. The cashiers can then adjust their behaviour accordingly. But this does not show that they have been fairly treated by the robber.

Ezorsky's requirement that the punishment of blameless offenders should not lead to their being falsely stigmatized as blameworthy cannot be met. As we have seen in Chapter 2, punishment is to be distinguished from other forms of infliction of suffering partly by the fact that punishment is the expression of blame or moral condemnation. This dimension of punishment may perhaps be ignored as minimal in cases where punishment is mild and takes the form of a fine. This is in fact the current position with respect to those strict liability offences known as public welfare offences—for example the selling of adulterated food. But Ezorsky's justification of strict liability is not confined to such cases. If the conditions she lays down are satisfied, then even the imprisonment of blameless offenders would be justified.[46] Nor is it realistic to insist

[46] Joel Feinberg discusses the differences between imprisonment for strict liability offences and fines for such offences. He argues that the former is clearly a form of punishment, whereas the latter may be a mere penalty, because 'imprisonment in modern times has taken on the symbolism of public reprobation'. See 'The Expressive Function of Punishment', in Hyman Gross and Andrew Von Hirsch (eds), *Sentencing* (New York, & Oxford, 1981), pp. 30–2.

that the punishment for strict liability offences should be confined to 'those involuntary offenders who are generally known
to be blameless'.[47] For if the offence is indeed a strict liability
offence, then the issue of whether the offender is really
blameworthy or not does not arise, and all who have committed
the legally prohibited act are liable to punishment. There is
no legal separation of the sheep from the goats, and for any
individual who is punished, the public can only make a
guess about his or her blameworthiness as the detailed circumstances under which the offence was committed will not be
publicly discussed and evaluated. So Ezorsky's point must
be the different one that there should be no *further* blame or
stigmatization.

But still, Ezorsky's conclusion is defensible—that under the
conditions described, the punishment of strict liability offenders is justified. She is also right in carefully distinguishing
her position from that of the utilitarian who would justify the
punishment of blameless offenders when the suffering inflicted
by such punishment is merely slightly less than the suffering
of the potential victims of crime.[48] My own earlier objections
to utilitarianism in Chapter 2 have already made it clear that
the utilitarian would justify the punishment of blameless offenders even when the suffering inflicted by punishment is much
greater than the suffering of each potential victim of crime,
provided that the aggregate of all the potential victims' suffering is at least slightly greater than the suffering caused by
punishment.

We may conclude from the above discussion that whereas
the punishment of negligent conduct is fair, strict liability
offences are unfair, although in exceptional situations their
unfairness may be overridden by other considerations.

5.3. *Wootton's System of Treatment*

Most defenders of strict liability only support strict liability
offences in particular cases, that is they support partial but
not total strict liability. However in her challenging book *Crime
and the Criminal Law,* Barbara Wootton makes a much more

---

[47] 'Punishment and Excuses', p. 102.
[48] Ibid., p. 112.

radical attack on what she takes to be the traditional approach
to the function of the criminal law.[49] According to her, on this
traditional view, the criminal law seeks to punish the wicked.[50]
This explains the rejection of strict liability offences, and the
law's requirement that *mens rea* is necessary for criminal conviction. For it is only when an offender commits a forbidden
act with *mens rea* that his action is considered wicked. Wootton
rejects the traditional view, and substitutes in its place the
very different view that the function of the criminal law is to
prevent socially harmful acts from occurring. These acts are
forbidden by the criminal law, and forbidden acts are committed not just by wicked people but also by those who are morally
blameless. For example, dangerous or careless driving causes
many deaths and injuries, and yet the offender 'seldom intends
the actual damage which he causes'.[51] But the harmful consequences of an act are the same whatever the mental state
of the offender. 'A man is equally dead and his relatives equally
bereaved whether he was stabbed or run over by a drunken
motorist or by an incompetent one; and the inconvenience
caused by the loss of your bicycle is unaffected by the question
whether or not the youth who removed it had the intention
of putting it back, if in fact he had not done so at the time of
his arrest.'[52] She points out that negligent, careless and indifferent acts cause more harm than acts done with deliberate
intent. Wootton therefore welcomes 'the multiplication of
offences of strict liability'.[53] The preventive system of treatment
that she envisages is one of total strict liability although she
acknowledges that there are problems with the implementation
of this system, and she does not propose the immediate
transfer of all crimes into the strict liability category.[54]

Wootton's system distinguishes between two stages, the conviction stage, and the sentencing or treatment stage. At the
conviction stage, *mens rea* is irrelevant and should not enter

[49] Barbara Wootton, *Crime and the Criminal Law*, Second edn., (London, 1981). This
edition includes Postscripts to each chapter. The postscripts incorporate some material
from her book *Crime and Penal Policy* (London, 1978).
[50] Ibid., p. 37.
[51] Ibid., p. 49.
[52] Ibid., p. 46.
[53] Ibid., p. 46.
[54] Ibid., p. 51.

into the definition of a crime. The issue to be determined at
this stage is whether the defendant is the person who did the
act prohibited by law. The question of whether the prohibited
act was done deliberately, recklessly, negligently, or accidentally is not relevant. So 'conviction' in this sense simply means
that there is sufficient evidence to show that the convicted
person has committed the forbidden act. It does not imply
that the offender is morally guilty or blameworthy. After conviction, the offender comes up for sentencing. At this stage,
mens rea is relevant, not in order to determine the degree of
responsibility or culpability of the offender for the crime, but
rather to help in determining the appropriate treatment of the
offender which will prevent a recurrence of the forbidden act.[55]
For example, the measures adopted for the prevention of accidental killing will differ from those needed to prevent deliberate
killing.

The aim of sentencing in the preventive system is 'to take
*the minimum action which offers an adequate prospect of preventing
future offences*'.[56] However, Wootton thinks that since we know
so little about the general deterrent effects of sentencing
the offender, we should, in choosing the type of treatment,
normally give priority to the likely effect of the treatment on
the offender himself.[57] This means that the primary function
of sentencing is to prevent recidivism.

For maximum effectiveness, Wootton favours indeterminate
sentences. The indeterminacy is both with respect to the duration of the sentence and the type of institution to which the
offender may be sent. The present sharp distinction between
penal institutions, in which offenders are punished, and medical institutions, in which the ill are treated, should be blurred
and ultimately eliminated altogether. Both institutions will
become 'places of safety' in which treatment is given to
offenders.[58] Opinions about the most suitable treatment for
particular offenders can be put to the test, and eventually
through systematic observation and experience, we can build
up a body of knowledge about the most appropriate treatment
for each type of offender.

[55] Ibid., pp. 48, 80.   [56] Ibid., p. 97. The emphasis is Wootton's.
[57] Ibid., p. 102.   [58] Ibid., p. 82.

Wotton maintains that her proposals do not depend on the truth of determinism. It is a fact that certain offenders respond to certain types of treatment and, according to her, it is not necessary to know whether they respond as a result of the exercise of free choice or because they could not have acted otherwise.[59] It should be pointed out that Wootton's case does not rely on the crude view that all criminal conduct is the product of illness. Nor does she have to deny that human beings are sometimes morally responsible for their actions. Her point is that evaluations of moral responsibility are not the concern of the criminal law whose aim is to prevent crime by treating offenders in ways which will prevent them from repeating prohibited acts.

I have so far outlined the alternative system of treatment that Wootton offers in place of the existing system of punishment, and I shall soon examine her arguments in favour of her system. But first, let us consider some initial objections to the practical operation of her scheme. Hers is a system of total strict liability, and it has sometimes been suggested that such a system of criminal law cannot work.

In his book on *Criminal Responsibility*, Francis G. Jacobs quotes an argument from Lon Fuller to the effect that in a system of total strict liability 'the conception of a causal connection between the act and the resulting injury would be lost'. Fuller writes:

A man in a drunken rage shoots his wife. Who among those concerned with this event share the responsibility for its occurrence—the killer himself, the man who lent the gun to him, the liquor dealer who provided the gin, or was it perhaps the friend who dissuaded him from securing a divorce that would have ended an unhappy alliance?[60]

Jacobs makes a number of acute criticisms of Fuller's argument. The most important of these is that questions of causation have nothing to do with strict liability. Jacobs is certainly right here: we can identify the person who is the cause of a harmful outcome without reference to the mental state of that person. When a person is thus picked out as the

---

[59] Ibid., pp. 80–1.
[60] Francis G. Jacobs, *Criminal Responsibility* (London, 1971), p. 148. The quotations are from Lon L. Fuller, *The Morality of Law* (New Haven, 1964).

cause of the harm, he is said to be causally responsible for it. But such attribution of causal responsibility is quite consistent with the guilt-denying framework of a system of total strict liability, for it does not impute moral blame or responsibility to the person. However, if the aim of the system of total strict liability is to prevent the occurrence of socially harmful acts, then it is not clear that attention should be confined to the causes of the acts, and not be extended also to all the causally relevant factors without which the harmful acts would not have occurred. Perhaps Fuller's point can be restated, not as the claim that it is impossible to identify the cause, but as the view that there are too many causally relevant factors to be dealt with. This seems to pose a dilemma for the definition of criminal acts in a system of total strict liability. *Either* the definition is manageably narrow to identify the person who is causally responsible for the harmful act, in which case we will be ignoring the possibility that the treatment of another person, who makes a causally relevant contribution to the occurrence of the harm, may be a more effective way of preventing the recurrence of the harm. *Or* the definition is sufficiently wide to allow for flexibility in the choice of who should be treated, in which case criminal conduct would be so broad that it captures in its net people engaging in all sorts of activities.

When Gertrude Ezorsky claims that total strict liability will be 'a utilitarian nightmare', she seems to have the latter alternative in mind:

The postal employees who unknowingly assist a bomb through the mail, the waiter who in ignorance serves poisoned coffee; they, together with the vast multitudes who unknowingly contribute causally to crime, would be implicated and punished as accessories. If a whole community unknowingly committed the offence of passing a counterfeit bill, everyone would land in jail.[61]

The point is perhaps exaggerated to the extent that in a system like Wootton's, treatment will not necessarily be given to all those who have made a causal contribution to the crime, but only to those whose treatment will best prevent the occurrence of the crime. None the less the quotation helps to bring out vividly the problems created by a broad definition of criminal conduct. The great loss of individual liberty and the wide use of discretionary powers by officials will be some of the inevitable consequences of adopting such a scheme.

A more limited problem about the definition of crime arises with respect to criminal attempts. Hart argues that socially harmful activities, like attempting to kill or injure or steal, can only be identified by reference to the intentions of offenders to produce the harmful consequences. So at least for these crimes, a reference to *mens rea* must be made in the definitions of the offences.[62] However, it has been suggested by Francis Jacobs that one can get round this problem by defining the offences in terms of 'general patterns of behaviour, and their typical tendencies, rather than in terms of the agent's knowledge, and his intention to produce certain consequences'.[63] Jacobs draws a useful analogy here with developments in the law of divorce which replaces the doctrine of matrimonial offence like desertion or cruelty, which requires evidence of intention, with the principle of breakdown of marriage.

So the practical difficulties faced by a system of total strict liability do not appear to be completely insurmountable, although getting round them involves a major sacrifice of individual liberty. But from a purely practical point of view, such a system cannot be killed off as easily as some might suppose, or hope.

I shall now consider Wootton's arguments for her proposal. A great part of her case consists in showing how the doctrine of *mens rea* has become both 'irrelevant and obstructive' in two types of situations—negligence in motoring offences, and the problem of the mentally abnormal offender.[64] I shall consider the case of negligence later in this chapter, but shall postpone the discussion of the mentally abnormal offender until the next chapter. It is important to note that even if Wootton's arguments go through in these two cases, they do not succeed in establishing her more general thesis that *mens rea* is completely irrelevant at the conviction stage. The two cases would only

---

[62] *Punishment and Responsibility*, p. 209.
[63] *Criminal Responsibility*, p. 146. Hart himself considers the possibility of defining the offence in terms of an act *likely* to have a certain harmful consequence. See *Punishment and Responsibility*, p. 264.
[64] *Crime and the Criminal Law*, p. 51.

support this thesis if it were shown that, for example, the proof of *mens rea* in all areas of the criminal law gives rise to the same kinds of intractable difficulties as in the two cases. This she does not attempt to show. But she seems to provide two more general arguments to support her thesis: (i) the impossibility of acquiring knowledge of other people's minds; and (ii) the rejection of the moral basis of *mens rea* as irrelevant to the prevention of crime.

(i) Wootton contends that 'it is not possible to get inside another man's skin'.[65] Although this view was stated in the context of discussing the problem of ascertaining whether mentally abnormal offenders could have resisted their desire to commit prohibited acts, it has presumably a wider application. Wootton does not provide an argument to support this general scepticism about our ability to know the mental states of others, and her view has been effectively criticized.[66] It is refuted by our daily experiences when we constantly conduct social relations, form plans, enter into agreements, and make judgements on the basis of our knowledge or beliefs about the intentions and attitudes of others. Sometimes our beliefs are mistaken, but there is no basis for suggesting that they must always be mistaken, or that, in the ordinary sense, we can never have the relevant knowledge. Of course Wootton's claim may be the weaker one that in practice it is nearly always very difficult to acquire knowledge of the mental states of others. But even this is not supported by our daily experiences. And in any case, the weaker claim is sufficient to create problems for her own system of treatment. At the sentencing or treatment stage, she herself has maintained that 'the presence or absence of guilty intention is all-important for its effect on the appropriate measures to be taken to prevent a recurrence of the forbidden act'.[67] This presupposes that it is possible to have knowledge of the offender's guilty intention, and if this knowledge can be acquired at the treatment stage, why is it not possible in general to obtain it at the earlier conviction stage? On the other hand, if the knowledge is really unavailable, then at the treatment

[65] Ibid., pp. 78, 90. See also *Crime and Penal Policy*, p. 228.
[66] See H. L. A. Hart, *Punishment and Responsibility*, pp. 202–3.
[67] *Crime and the Criminal Law*, pp. 47–8.

stage we lack a vital piece of information necessary for effective treatment.[68]

The practical difficulties of proving the presence of *mens rea* have often been used as an argument favouring strict liability. Although in a particular case this argument may well be decisive,[69] it cannot plausibly be applied generally to support a system of treatment like Wootton's. For whatever practical advantages are gained at the conviction stage will be outweighed by the problems of devising suitable safeguards at the treatment stage. A system of indeterminate treatment allows flexibility for offenders to be moved from one form of treatment to another, and can therefore give rise to grave potential abuses against which careful safeguards must be constructed. Wootton herself subscribes to the moral judgement that 'freedom to live one's life after the fashion of one's choice is of value in itself',[70] and this freedom is unjustifiably undermined in a preventive system if offenders are kept longer than necessary. Freedom, and the respect we owe to offenders as fellow human beings capable of exercising control over their own lives, demand that offenders should not be subjected to unjustified experiments by experts with new, or even old, and untested theories which involve longer confinements or more unpleasant conditions of confinement. Regular reviews by independent bodies would be necessary. The setting up and operation of such bodies, and the other inquiries needed to provide a rational basis for treatment, will create practical and administrative problems which will make the practical difficulties of proving *mens rea* before conviction seem simple by comparison.[71]

(ii) The most important general argument that Wootton gives in support of her system of treatment is that which renounces what she takes to be the whole moral basis of *mens rea* as irrelevant to the purpose of crime prevention. She

[68] See Richard A. Wasserstrom, 'H. L. A. Hart and the Doctrines of *Mens Rea* and Criminal Responsibility', p. 120.
[69] See the discussion in the next chapter of whether an offender had an 'irresistible impulse' to commit a criminal act.
[70] *Crime and the Criminal Law*, p. 97.
[71] See Joel Feinberg's comments in 'Crime, Clutchability, and Individuated Treatment', in Jeffrie G. Murphy (ed.), *Punishment and Rehabilitation* (Belmont, 1973), pp. 228–9, 232–4.

presents us with a stark choice between a punitive system designed to punish the wicked, and a preventive system whose function is to prevent the occurrence of socially harmful acts prohibited by the criminal law. She asserts that it is only within the former system that *mens rea* has a place in confining conviction and punishment to wicked offenders. She traces the moral basis of *mens rea* to a retributive theory of punishment which dictates not merely that only the wicked, that is those who acted with *mens rea*, should be punished, but also that the severity of punishment should depend on the moral deserts of offenders. Within such a punitive system the preventive function will only be served incidentally and in a rather haphazard manner.

Our discussion of Hart's rationale of legal excuses has shown why the choice that Wootton presents is a false one. It is quite consistent to insist with Hart that society needs a 'moral licence' to punish which sets fair terms to individuals, while at the same time recognizing that the purpose of having such a licence is at least generally to prevent crime. A constraint on the pursuit of the preventive function of the criminal law seems to be present even within Wootton's system. As we have just noted, she subscribes to the value of individual freedom, and should not therefore be prepared to sacrifice any amount of the offender's freedom just in order to secure a slightly lower risk of recidivism. There are measures, like the widespread invasions of privacy, which we are unwilling to use even though their adoption will further the goal of crime prevention. So, in the same spirit, acceptance of the preventive function of the criminal law does not imply that we should sweep aside the requirements of *mens rea* at the conviction stage, for these requirements ensure that offenders are not unfairly used for the benefit of society. It is therefore a serious mistake on Wootton's part to think that if we reject her system of treatment then we must be opting for a crude punitive system in which the prevention of crime is only an incidental by-product of the system whose central aim is to punish the wicked.

But perhaps the constraints on using offenders for the benefit of society only apply when we are *punishing* them, and not, as in Wootton's scheme, when we are *treating* them. It has been pointed out that we use people for the benefit of society when we quarantine carriers of infectious diseases, for 'it is clear both that the only reason for doing so is the protection of others and that the person is not responsible for being a carrier'.[72] There is of course a difference in that Wootton's system of treatment involves greater interferences with people's lives both because of the wide range of conduct which it covers, and because of the tests and inquiries which it permits in order to discover the appropriate forms of treatment. But there are also much more important moral differences between her system and the practice of quarantining carriers of infectious diseases.

When we punish blameless offenders, we perpetrate a special injustice on them because in punishing them we are expressing our moral condemnation of them. We discussed this in the previous section in connection with partial strict liability offences. Now we are confronted with a system of total strict liability in which treatment has replaced punishment, and it might seem that the issue of fairness is no longer relevant. However, this is not so, and some of the considerations already raised earlier will appear again in a different form.

Wootton's system of treatment is unlike quarantine or the civil commitment of the dangerous insane in which all who are detained are known not to be culpable for their undesirable condition. On the other hand, even though the issue of culpability is irrelevant in Wootton's system, our general experience and knowledge of our own and others' conduct will lead us to infer that some offenders are culpable while others are not, though we will not be able to place particular offenders into one category or the other. So we know that some who broke laws meant for social protection did so intentionally, while others had unrecognized excuses. And yet in Wootton's system it is possible that some of the former will be released because no treatment is thought to be necessary, while some of the latter will be detained for long periods of treatment.[73] Both categories of offenders may be equally used for the benefit of society. I suggest that it is unfair to treat in this manner

[72] Richard A. Wasserstrom, 'H. L. A. Hart and the Doctrines of *Mens Rea* and Criminal Responsibility', p. 121.
[73] Wasserstrom draws attention to some of the radical implications of Wootton's scheme, ibid., pp. 118–20.

those who had unrecognized excuses. However, the merits of this suggestion are obscured by Wootton's scepticism about the general deterrent effect of harsh treatment. So let us now consider cases in which this general deterrent effect cannot be ignored in a preventive system.

Indeed Wootton herself dealt with one such case when she presided over a juvenile court in which a youth of 16, with a previously unblemished record, was charged with rape though with mitigating circumstances. 'The girl had apparently at first led the boy on, but when later she tried to get out of it, he threatened her with a knife and got his way.'[74] The offender had been 'thoroughly frightened' to discover that the maximum sentence for rape was life imprisonment, but the bench was confident that he would not repeat the offence, and issued a probation order. The probation officer shared the bench's confidence, but confided privately that 'the news will soon go round on the grapevine that you can do what you like with a girl'.[75] Here is a case which, if the probation officer was right, a preventive system of treatment would have imposed an exemplary sentence. There are probably also many other cases in which serious harm is done by persons who are most unlikely to repeat their offences, but whose harsh treatment is needed to deter potential offenders. For example, some of those who kill are unlikely to do so again. In all these cases if we treat offenders by subjecting them to a long period of confinement, then we are using them for the benefit of society. Surely we use them unfairly if they lacked the capacity or opportunity to conform to the law. And yet from the purely preventive point of view, given the equal unlikelihood of recidivism, it makes no difference whether we use a deliberate offender for the purposes of general deterrence or choose instead an offender with an excuse. The general deterrent effects of such harsh treatment will not depend on who is subjected to the treatment as all crimes in Wootton's scheme are strict liability offences, and the general public will be unaware of the mental states of offenders.

When an offender with an unrecognized excuse is used in this manner for the benefit of society, we add insult to the

[74] *Crime and Penal Policy*, p. 38.
[75] Ibid., p. 39.

injury that we inflict on him. For he, who lacked control over his offending act, is compulsorily treated in order to prevent others, who have such control over their actions, from committing harmful acts. This insult is absent both in the case of quarantine, and in the case of the civil commitment of the insane who are detained in order to prevent themselves, and not others, from causing harm in future.

So even when the treatment of offenders is distinguished from punishment, issues of fairness cannot be disregarded. However, the blurring, and eventual elimination, of the distinction between prison and hospital, which Wootton hopes for, may not come about. Prisons have a long history as punitive institutions, while hospitals will continue to treat non-offenders who are ill, and people will have difficulty in seeing both institutions as performing the same function with respect to offenders. And if the distinction between them remains, then most of those who are treated in prison are likely to be regarded by the community at large as deserving of moral condemnation, and their treatment will acquire some of the features of punishment. Although in Wootton's system the law will ignore the mental elements of crime at the conviction stage, these mental elements will, as we saw earlier, continue to be of crucial importance in what Hart calls 'a society of persons'. People will want to distinguish between offenders who have an excuse and those who don't. If the law does not provide them with a reliable basis for the distinction, then folklore is likely to give unreliable guidance.

I shall now briefly comment on Wootton's account of driving offences which is one of the areas in which she thinks that the doctrine of *mens rea* is 'irrelevant and obstructive'. She points to the grave harm done by driving offences, and argues that many of these offences can only be dealt with by the criminal courts on the basis of strict liability. Driving offenders seldom intend to cause the damage they inflict. The damage is often done 'by negligence, or by indifference to the welfare of others' rather than by 'deliberate wickedness'.[76] But her whole argument here is vitiated by the very narrow conception of *mens rea* that she adopts. It is quite clear that much of the damage

[76] *Crime and the Criminal Law*, p. 50.

she has in mind is done by drivers who are reckless or negligent, and both recklessness and negligence should properly be included in *mens rea*.[77] We have already seen that there is a moral distinction between negligence and strict liability. To make negligent driving a criminal offence is not to adopt strict liability.

The real problem of driving offences lies elsewhere as indeed Wootton's own writings amply illustrate. In *Crime and Penal Policy*, she marshalls impressive facts and figures to back up her claims that motorists are responsible for 'enormous social injury and damage' and that they have 'scant respect for the law'.[78] It is enough to mention just one piece of evidence from England and Wales: 'In 1975, 486 persons were found guilty of causing death by dangerous driving, as against 107 convicted of murder and 369 of either murder or manslaughter.'[79] And yet, as she further points out, 'motoring convictions are only too effectively destigmatized by current social attitudes'.[80] They are not treated as 'real crimes'. Where offenders are disqualified from driving, this is often regarded as similar to a failure to qualify for a certain profession, or as professional misconduct rather than a criminal act. Where they are fined, they can well afford it, and treat it as a form of tax rather than as punishment. She shows that the law itself facilitates the destigmatization of motoring offences by allowing certain types of offenders to plead guilty through the post, thus avoiding the necessity of appearing in court.[81]

Wootton speculates that 'the tendency to "play down" motoring offences is not unconnected with the fact that they are more commonly committed by persons of superior social status than are other types of crime'.[82] That is perhaps the crux of the problem. But it is hard to see how the wholesale adoption of strict liability in motoring offences can do anything but harden the present social attitude of treating motoring offences as not really criminal.

[77] In one place she refers to negligence as 'a watered down version of *mens rea*'. See *Crime and the Criminal Law*, p. 45.
[78] *Crime and Penal Policy*, p. 211.
[79] Ibid., p. 212.
[80] Ibid., p. 209.
[81] Ibid., pp. 209–10.
[82] *Crime and the Criminal Law*, p. 28. See also *Crime and Penal Policy*, pp. 206–7.

6

MENTALLY ILL OFFENDERS

6.1. *Legal Insanity*

MENTALLY ill offenders pose special problems for the criminal law. As Lady Wootton points out, the issue of mental illness may be raised at three different stages.[1] First, the accused may be certified insane and therefore unfit to stand trial. Secondly, the accused may plead mental illness as an excuse to a criminal charge, or, as in the case of the English Homicide Act 1957, the accused may enter a plea of 'diminished responsibility' in order to reduce a charge of murder to that of manslaughter. Thirdly, when an offender has been convicted, the court may substitute medical for penal treatment.[2]

Again even when the accused successfully pleads the defence of mental illness to a criminal charge, this does not necessarily result in his being discharged. He may still be detained for medical treatment. The most well-known recent case of this is that of Hinckley who shot President Reagan and three other people, but was acquitted in 1982 on the grounds of insanity, and then committed to a hospital. In this respect the excuse of mental illness is unlike other excuses which, when successfully pleaded, set the accused free.

According to the McNaghten Rules of 1843, in order to establish a defence of insanity it must be proved that the accused 'was labouring under such a defect of reason, from disease of the mind, as not to know the nature and quality of the act he was doing; or, if he did know it, that he did not know he was doing what was wrong'.

The McNaghten Rules can be given a narrow or a broad interpretation. Even on the narrowest interpretation, it would cover cases of delusions which are so gross that the offender who does something harmful thinks that he is doing something

[1] Barbara Wootton, *Crime and Penal Policy* (London, 1978), p. 227.
[2] Other ways in which the issue of mental illness is relevant under English criminal law are discussed by Wootton in *Crime and the Criminal Law*. Second edn., (London, 1981), pp 68–71.

quite harmless. An example often cited is that of a person who strangles another person thinking that he is squeezing an orange or a lemon.[3] Such a person literally does not 'know the nature and quality of the act he was doing'. But such cases rarely occur. If therefore they are the only type of case to pass the McNaghten test of insanity, then that test would be far too narrow. It would not even cover the two famous cases of crime committed by those suffering from delusions.

The first case is that which led to the framing of the McNaghten Rules. Daniel McNaghten, suffering from the paranoid delusion that the Prime Minister, Sir Robert Peel, was part of the plot to persecute and to destroy him, shot at and killed Peel's secretary believing him to be Peel. The second case, which took place even earlier, in 1800, is that of Hadfield whose delusion was that he was in constant communication with God and that, like Christ, he had to sacrifice himself for the salvation of the world. He fired his pistol at King George III but did not hit him.[4]

Although McNaghten knew that his act was one of killing, there is a broader sense in which he did not know or appreciate 'the nature and quality' of his act. It was not for him an act of killing an innocent person. Because of his delusion, he regarded his act as one of self-defence. What is important here is not simply that his belief was false, but rather that the belief was a symptom of his paranoia which incapacitated him from correcting and adjusting his belief in the light of the true situation. Again, an ordinary offender might be expected to distinguish between a situation in which there is an immediate threat to his life, and one in which there is a plot to kill him at some stage. But there is no reason to believe that McNaghten had the capacity to distinguish between those situations in which there was no alternative but to kill in self-defence, and other situations in which various evasive actions to save one's life might be taken.

In Hadfield's case there is also a sense in which he knew

[3] See, for example, David A. J. Richards, *The Moral Criticism of Law* (Encino & Belmont, 1977), p. 210; and Anthony Kenny, 'The Expert in Court', *The Law Quarterly Review*, 99 (1983), p. 212.

[4] These two cases are discussed in interesting detail by Herbert Fingarette, *The Meaning of Criminal Insanity* (Berkeley & Los Angeles, 1974), pp. 128–58, and esp. pp. 138–40. I am much indebted to his analysis of these cases, as indeed to the whole book.

what he was doing, for he intended to shoot at the King, and he was capable of planning his course of action. But he saw his act as carrying out God's will, and as an act of sacrifice for the salvation of the human race. While in the grip of his delusion he was incapable of regarding his act as wrong.

The McNaghten Rules should therefore be given a broader interpretation to cover cases like those of Daniel McNaghten and Hadfield. But I do not know how best to formulate the test in order to give effect to this broader interpretation. It would appear that something like the version proposed by the American Law Institute's Model Penal Code would be helpful. This states that, 'A person is not responsible for criminal conduct if at the time of such conduct as a result of mental disease or defect he lacks substantial capacity either to appreciate the criminality (or wrongfulness) of his conduct or to conform his conduct to the requirement of law.'[5] In Australia, where the McNaghten test is given a fairly wide interpretation, a useful gloss was placed by Chief Justice Dixon in a 1933 case on the meaning of 'know the wrongness' of the act done. Dixon asked whether the accused could 'think rationally of the reasons which to ordinary people make that act right or wrong'. 'If through the disordered condition of his mind he could not reason about the matter with a moderate degree of sense and composure it may be said that he could not know that what he was doing was wrong.'[6]

The broader interpretation would still not satisfy those critics who proclaim that the McNaghten test of insanity is one which can only identify cognitive impairments. They argue that there are serious forms of mental illness which involve non-cognitive impairments. A person might know that he was performing a wrongful act and yet lack the capacity to control his conduct in conformity with the law. It is often said that some mentally ill persons suffer from an 'irresistible impulse' to commit certain criminal acts.

However, even when the legal test for insanity is broadened further to include an irresistible impulse test, it is still unacceptable to those who believe that mental illness should be a defence

[5] Quoted by Herbert Fingarette, ibid., p. 13.
[6] Quoted by Herbert Fingarette, ibid., p. 204 n. 17. For a useful account of the relevant Australian laws, see Ivan Potas, *Just Deserts for the Mad* (Canberra, 1982).

to a criminal charge in a more fundamental way. Thus the Report of the Committee on Mentally Abnormal Offenders (the Butler Report) recommended that a special verdict of 'not guilty on evidence of mental disorder' should be returned 'if at the time of the act or omission charged the defendant was suffering from severe mental illness or severe subnormality'.[7] But this seems to go too far in excusing the severely mentally ill. For even in cases of severe mental illness, a person's illness does not necessarily affect his conduct in all areas of his life, but may be confined to certain actions. He can therefore be held responsible for some of his acts while he is not responsible for others.

As Fingarette points out, 'A defect in capacity of rational conduct may appear in one area of conduct more than others, for example, in relation to food, sex, high places, or religion. The defect may manifest itself continuously or only from time to time, with interludes of sanity.'[8] Fingarette also quotes the following remarks of a forensic psychiatrist: 'No matter how unfounded or absurd his delusions, the paranoiac may retain an appearance of normality and react in normal fashion to matters outside his delusional system.'[9] In this respect, the mentally ill are therefore very different from very young children or the mentally retarded who are not accorded the status of responsible moral agents, and are not therefore criminally liable for any of their acts.

The fact that a person is mentally ill at the time of his offence does not in itself show that his illness is causally connected with the offence. Perhaps the absence of a connection is most unlikely in some cases. For example, although a person suffering from a delusion may be capable of conducting himself normally in areas outside his 'delusional system' it may none the less be the case that his delusion so dominates his life that he is unlikely to do anything of significance unless this is in

[7] Home Office, Department of Health and Social Security, *Report of the Committee on Mentally Abnormal Offenders*, HMSO Cmnd. 6244 (London, 1975), para. 18.30. See also paras. 18.17, 18.29. The Report goes on to define 'severe mental illness' in para. 18. 35.

[8] *The Meaning of Criminal Insanity*, op. cit., pp. 204–5. I am not sure how this acknowledgement is compatible with Fingarette's view that 'insanity and childhood both preclude responsibility status, and they therefore preclude moral judgements and legal judgements of criminality' (p. 141).   [9] Ibid., p. 209 fn. 23.

some way connected with his delusion. But while this may be true, it is not something that we can simply assume to be the case without further investigation. The point here is well illustrated by an example given by Kenny.[10] Suppose that an academic suffers from paranoid delusions that his work of genius is being plagiarized by his colleagues who also unjustly deny him his promotion. If the academic secretly poisons his mother-in-law in order to inherit her large fortune, this act is not connected with his delusions and so should not excuse him from criminal liability.

But Kenny goes further to argue that even when there is a connection between his crime and the mental illness, he should not be exempt from criminal responsibility unless his act was not wrong had his beliefs been true. Thus Kenny argues that if the academic kills the head of his department for not promoting him, he should not be excused because even if his beliefs were not delusionary but true, the killing would not be justified. However, this further point is somewhat dubious. For once so strong a connection with his delusions has been established, it is doubtful that the mentally ill person is capable of seeing the significance of different responses to the personal injustice, and of acting in proportion to the wrong done to him. Gross, commenting on a similar view as Kenny's which was enunciated in one of the original McNaghten Rules, observes: 'It holds that a person whose insanity consists merely in delusions is still capable of choosing to act in conformity with the law governing the situation as he perceive it . . . According to the better medical knowledge available now, however, the fact of the matter is that such persons in the grip of their delusions are normally so severely incapacitated that they cannot even choose to act otherwise.'[11]

If we reject the idea that severe mental illness at the time of the crime is in itself sufficient to exempt from criminal liability, then we have to consider whether tests of legal insanity, consisting of a combination of the McNaghten Rules and the 'irresistible impulse' rule, are adequate. It is here that we have to return to Lady Wootton's objections.

[10] Anthony Kenny, 'The Expert in Court', p. 212. See also his *Freewill and Responsibility* (London, 1978), pp. 81–2.
[11] Hyman Gross, *A Theory of Criminal Justice* (New York, 1979), p. 308.

6.2. *The Abolition of the Insanity Defence?*

Wootton contends that we are not competent to differentiate between the wicked and the sick because we lack the ability to acquire knowledge of the mental states of offenders. She directs her attack in particular against the claim that, because of mental illness, a particular offender is subjected to an irresistible impulse or temptation to commit the prohibited act, or that he suffered from diminished responsibility. She also strongly rejects the view that psychopaths (or sociopaths), who persistently engage in anti-social behaviour, do so because of a mental disorder or illness.

Much of what she says is wholly persuasive. For example, she maintains that the cause of persistent criminal conduct cannot be identified with the criminal conduct itself for which it is the cause. So if psychopathic disorder is the cause, then it must have some identifiable symptoms of its own which are distinct from the persistent criminal conduct.[12] When therefore the only facts available to the court are the offender's persistent criminal conduct, there is no basis to conclude that the offender is suffering from a mental illness which should exempt him from criminal responsibility. It is a fallacy to assume that 'criminal responsibility disappears when criminality is sufficiently persistent, serious and intractable'.[13]

Similarly, when we leave aside her more extravagant claims about the impossibility of knowing the mental states of another person, Wootton presents a very strong case to show the practical difficulties of determining in a court of law whether an offender is subject to an irresistible impulse or temptation, or whether he should succeed in his plea for diminished responsibility as a result of mental illness. She maintains that juries do not understand the 'sophisticated subtleties' of legal disputations in this area and tend to reach their conclusions on simpler grounds.[14] Thus they are likely to think that if an accused had a history of mental instability then his responsibility for his crime is impaired. She also points out that from the fact that an impulse has not been resisted, we cannot conclude that it could not be resisted. In practice there is no

---

[12] *Crime and Penal Policy*, p. 232.
[13] Ibid., p. 232.
[14] *Crime and the Criminal Law*, p. 76.

way of distinguishing between an irresistible temptation and a temptation that was simply not resisted. People tend to assume that bizarre desires, or desires which seem pointless or exceptionally revolting to the ordinary person, are more powerful and more difficult to resist than familiar desires and temptations.[15] Wootton observes that our attitudes towards criminal conduct is paradoxical: 'if a man's crimes are by ordinary standards only moderately objectionable, we are prepared to regard him as wicked, and therefore a suitable subject for punishment; but if his wickedness goes beyond a certain point, it ceases to be wickedness at all and becomes mental disorder'.[16]

This last remark is not entirely accurate. In two recent multiple murder cases in England of a particularly gruesome kind, pleas of diminished responsibility were unsuccessfully made. In 1981, Sutcliffe was convicted of murdering 13 women. In some cases he had sadistically mutilated his victims. 'Sutcliffe gave an elaborate account of his belief in a personal divine mission to purify society by killing prostitutes (the last group of his victims were not in fact prostitutes), and his defending counsel summoned the evidence of three psychiatrists who testified to the truthfulness of the accused's description of his mental state and confirmed their diagnosis of paranoid schizophrenia.'[17] In the second case, Nilsen confessed to having killed 15 men. He had cut up their bodies, buried some pieces in his garden, placed some in plastic bags which were kept in his cupboards and wardrobes, and even flushed some pieces down the toilet.[18] He was convicted on six counts of murder and two of attempted murder. Some of his victims were beyond identification.

But none the less Wootton presents a sufficiently convincing case against the irresistible impulse defence and the plea of diminished responsibility. However, this case seems to leave

[15] *Crime and Penal Policy*, p. 229.

[16] Ibid., p. 231.

[17] Peter Sedgwick, 'Antipsychiatry from the Sixties and Eighties', in Walter R. Gove (ed.), *Deviance and Mental Illness* (Beverly Hills, 1982), p. 219. Sedgwick gives an interesting discussion of the case against the background of the experiment in the United States in which nine pseudopatients succeeded in deceiving psychiatrists into diagnosing them as schizophrenic by feigning auditory hallucinations.

[18] See Brian Masters, *Killing for Company: the Case of Dennis Nilsen* (London, 1985).

untouched the McNaghten test of legal insanity. Indeed Wootton contrasts the vagueness of the notion of diminished responsibility with the precision of the test of legal insanity provided by the McNaghten Rules. However, she thinks that in order to satisfy the McNaghten test, 'a man would indeed have to be far out of touch with reality, and it might be difficult to convince a jury that he had been so completely out of his mind'.[19] The most common criticisms of the McNaghten Rules denounce the narrowness of the Rules, but not the practical difficulties of their application. These criticisms can to some extent be met by adopting a broader interpretation of the McNaghten test as discussed in the previous section.

Wootton therefore succeeds in undermining some, but not all, the tests for legal insanity. The McNaghten test survives her specific charges against the use of the irresistible impulse test and the plea for diminished responsibility. (So indeed does the recommendation of the Butler Report, considered earlier, that offenders with severe mental illnesses, which are defined, should be excused if they were suffering from such illnesses at the time of their offences.) Her case for the total elimination of the excuse of mental illness must therefore stand or fall with her more general case for a wholly preventive system of criminal law based on total strict liability. But that general case has already been considered and rejected in the previous chapter. So her case for the total abolition of the insanity defence falls. If the doctrine of *mens rea* is defensible, as I have argued that it is, then one is not justified in completely excluding mental illness as a legal excuse, and some test for legal insanity should be retained.

A mentally ill person, who satisfies the McNaghten test, might not know the nature of his act, and would therefore lack the *mens rea* necessary for criminal liability. Mental illness involving cognitive impairments can deprive persons of the knowledge and intention relevant to the proof of *mens rea*.[20] So, on the one hand, it is important that such persons should not be convicted and punished just as other offenders who lack

[19] *Crime and Penal Policy*, p. 141.
[20] See H. L. A. Hart, *Punishment and Responsibility* (Oxford, 1968), p. 206 n.; and Joel Feinberg, 'Crime, Clutchability, and Individuated Treatment', in Jeffrie G. Murphy (ed.), *Punishment and Rehabilitation* (Belmont, 1973), pp. 231–2.

mens rea are not convicted or punished. But on the other hand, it is also important that mentally ill offenders who acted without *mens rea* should not be automatically released in the same way that other offenders who are excused are released. A mentally ill offender lacking *mens rea* may cause serious harm to others if he is immediately released without medical treatment. Mental illness should therefore be a distinct excuse different from other excuses. When a mentally ill person is acquitted but is detained for medical treatment, he is not being punished, and should not therefore be detained in a penal institution. His position is now like that of mentally ill persons who are subjected to involuntary civil commitment in order to prevent them from harming others.[21]

Mental illness should excuse not only when it directly deprives the accused of *mens rea*, but also when it so incapacitates him that his intentions and plans are merely responses to his delusions. A mentally ill person who has the intention to kill can take careful steps to carry out that intention, and change his plans in the service of that intention. But the intention itself is a product of the delusion, and is not something he is capable of revising while he is suffering from the delusion. His delusion makes him unable to see the wrongness of the act, and makes it seem the only way of reacting to his perceived situation. In such cases, intentions and knowledge of the consequences of one's actions do not carry the weight of responsibility that they normally do. The general principle supporting the doctrine of *mens rea*, and explicated in the previous chapter, that people should not be liable to punishment if they did not have the capacity and fair opportunity to conform to the law, applies as much here as it does with respect to other legal excuses.[22]

The suggestion that the test of legal insanity should be confined to a version of the McNaghten Rules and not include

---

[21] These points are well made by Ivan Potas, *Just Deserts for the Mad*, p. 59.

[22] Thomas Szasz has argued to the opposite conclusion that mental illness is 'a myth' which is used to hide a person's responsibility for his other actions. A brief, but forceful and quite representative, statement of Szasz's view can be found in 'The Myth of Mental Illness' in Jeffrie G. Murphy (ed.), *Punishment and Rehabilitation*. For criticisms of Szasz, see Michael S. Moore, *Law and Psychiatry* (Cambridge, 1984), esp. Ch. 4. See also Peter Sedgwick, *Psycho Politics* (London, 1982), Ch. 6, and Leslie Stevenson, 'Mind, Brain and Mental Illness', *Philosophy*, 52 (1977).

the test of irresistible impulse will be attacked for not giving recognition to those forms of mental illnesses involving non-cognitive impairments. To this two replies may be made.

First, the problem is the practical one of formulating a legal test of insanity that can be effectively applied by a jury in a court-room. The irresistible impulse test seems to fall apart under Wootton's onslaught. But I do not go so far as Kenny who maintains that the notion of irresistible impulse is 'an incoherent piece of nonsense', and hence the accused cannot have acted on such an impulse 'any more than he can have murdered a married bachelor or stolen a square circle'.[23] For consider a typical case of addiction in which a person tries to give up drinking but fails. If he has tried sufficiently hard, he might be led by these efforts to declare that he had an 'irresistible desire' to drink, and to seek treatment to overcome it. What gives sense to his claim in this context are his sincere dissociation from his drinking habit, the evident distress it causes him, and his known attempts to break the habit. Similarly we can make sense of the kleptomaniac's compulsion to steal and treat it as 'irresistible' if the objects stolen are of no value to him, and he knows that the probability of apprehension is not only very great but will also cause him a lot of distress. Consider now the case of an offender who kills. Under ideal conditions of observing his behaviour, and in the absence of doubt about the sincerity of his own declarations, we see him disturbed before the killing, confessing to having homicidalcidal desires which he does not understand or identify with, and seeking help. When he kills, there is no motive, no interest of his which is served by the killing, and there is only remorse and total confusion that he should have committed such an act. It is as if the impulse to kill is like an alien force with a life of its own while he is merely a helpless spectator having no control over it. Under these circumstances we can indeed say that he had an 'irresistible impulse' to kill.

But of course the conditions under which we are in a position to make such a judgement of the offender are hardly those which obtain in the court-room. There the offender's account of his own mental states is given in the context where he has a strong interest in establishing the presence of an excuse, and

[23] 'The Expert in Court', p. 210.

cannot therefore be freely accepted. There may be no basis for determining whether he could have resisted the desire to kill.

The second reply to the objection that the McNaghten test of insanity ignores non-cognitive impairments, is that we cannot separate so sharply cognitive and non-cognitive impairments. If a broad version of the McNaghten test is used, then, as our earlier discussion already indicates, this will also capture some non-cognitive incapacities.[24] But of course the McNaghten test will not capture the whole range of non-cognitive incapacities. We are back to the problem of devising a suitable test of legal insanity which, like the McNaghten test, can be fairly easily applied, but which at the same time captures more of the excusing incapacities of mentally ill offenders. At present there does not seem to be such a test. So it has to be admitted that we can only raise two cheers for the McNaghten test.

Under the notion of legal insanity provided by a broad interpretation of the McNaghten Rules, there will be some mentally ill offenders who are not excused. Their mental illness at the time of the offence may provide a mitigation reducing the sentence they would otherwise have received.[25] Their mental illness at the time of the sentence will be relevant in ascertaining the most suitable form of punishment— whether, for example, they should be detained in a special hospital. But mitigating factors can have the effect of reducing sentences only when there is no mandatory punishment for an offence. My suggestion that the plea of diminished responsibility should be abolished means that a mentally ill offender will no longer be able to use this plea to reduce a charge of murder to that of manslaughter. If murder still carries a mandatory life sentence, then mentally ill offenders convicted of

---

[24] See also Kenny's comment: 'Will is the capacity to behave in pursuit of long-term goals and in the light of the comparative attractiveness of alternative courses of action: because of this, an investigation of an agent's ability to understand what he is doing and its relevance to long-term goals, and his judgements of comparative value, is not something distinct from, or irrelevant to, an inquiry into the effectiveness of his will', *Freewill and Responsibility*, p. 44.

[25] For helpful comments on the sentencing of mentally ill offenders, see Norval Morris, *Madness and the Criminal Law* (Chicago & London, 1982), Ch. 4; and Ivan Potas, *Just Deserts for the Mad*, Ch. 10.

murder will not be able to get a reduced sentence. It is therefore an implication of the argument of this section that murder should not carry a mandatory sentence, nor indeed should any other offence.

6.3. *Dangerousness*

It is sometimes suggested that dangerous offenders pose a special problem in that it may be desirable to punish them more severely than would otherwise be justified just in order to prevent them from harming others in future. The issue has gained in importance for a variety of reasons. Some think that focusing on dangerous offenders can be an effective way of controlling crime.[26] Others believe that the social climate may soon be hospitable to the passing of generally shorter sentences. But when this happens, it is argued that the protection of society from the small number of dangerous offenders will require the introduction of a special protective sentence.[27] When long prison sentences for all serious offenders are thought to be justified on, for example, retributive grounds, no special problem arises for the minority of dangerous offenders because the long sentences would be sufficient in any case to prevent them from repeating their offences. But if shorter sentences for serious offenders are acceptable, then attention will have to be paid to dangerous offenders who are still likely to commit grave offences after serving the shorter sentences.[28]

The issue, thus presented, is of course one which affects both dangerous offenders who are mentally ill as well as those who are not. But the problem is particularly acute for mentally ill offenders because it is often assumed that they are more

[26] See Mark H. Moore, Susan R. Estrich, Daniel McGillis and William Spelman, *Dangerous Offenders: The Elusive Target of Justice* (Cambridge, 1984).

[27] See Jean Floud and Warren Young, *Dangerousness and Criminal Justice* (London, 1981), hereafter referred to as the Floud Report; and Jean Floud, 'Dangerousness and Criminal Justice', *British Journal of Criminology*, 22, no. 3 (1982). This issue of the journal is a special number on Dangerousness, and, apart from the article by Floud, there are several other valuable papers, especially those by A. E. Bottoms and Roger Brownsword, 'The Dangerousness Debate after the Floud Report', Ted Honderich, 'On Justifying Protective Punishment', and Nigel Walker, 'Unscientific, Unwise, Unprofitable or Unjust?'.

[28] See Jean Floud, 'Dangerousness and Criminal Justice', pp. 216–17. She also points out that the provision of a special protective sentence 'may well be a condition of securing shorter sentences overall' (p. 215).

dangerous than other offenders, and if their preventive detention takes the form of subjecting them to treatment in a hospital
rather than ordinary imprisonment, then this is regarded as
more easily justifiable. The sentence of life imprisonment has
often been used as a preventive measure for mentally ill offenders who have committed grave offences and are thought likely
to do so again in future. Thus speaking of the situation in
England and Wales, D. A. Thomas observes that the life sentence is 'reserved for persons who have committed offences of
substantial gravity and who appear to be suffering from some
disorder of personality or instability of character which makes
them likely to commit grave offences in the future if left at
large or released from a fixed term of imprisonment. The
sentence is not normally used as a tariff sentence to deal with
offenders of normal mentality who have committed offences
of grave gravity.'[29] But Thomas also cites a case in which an
offender was sentenced to life imprisonment for 'robbery consisting of the theft of two pounds from a man accosted in the
street and threatened with an air pistol'.[30] Medical evidence
was given suggesting that the offender's limited ability to control his 'abnormally high sexual drive' would very probably
lead to his commission of violent sexual offences if he were
released, and it was also thought that there was no prospect
of an effective treatment.

    From the utilitarian point of view, there is no problem in
imposing a protective sentence on an offender if we are certain
that this would prevent him from committing a serious offence
and the harm that would be caused by the offence is greater
than the harm of the punishment. Part of the utilitarian
justification of punishment is to incapacitate the offender. But
protective sentencing raises an acute problem of justice
because, at least at the present state of our knowledge, the
predictions of dangerousness are not very reliable. As Norval
Morris points out, there are two false positive predictions for
every one true positive prediction, that is for every one correct
prediction that an offender will commit a violent crime if he
were released, there are two cases in which such predictions
are false.[31] The Floud Report accepts that the false positive

[29] D. A. Thomas, *Principles of Sentencing*, Second edn., (London, 1982), p. 301.
[30] Ibid., p. 305.   [31] *Madness and the Criminal Law*, p. 165.

rate for predictions of serious violence is at least 50 per cent.[32] Nigel Walker agrees that 'we have not succeeded in providing criteria which would ensure that a predication of future violence would be right more often than it would be wrong. With present criteria, it would more often be wrong.'[33] However, he thinks it likely that much greater predictive accuracy can be achieved, and in a later contribution, he suggests that it is now possible 'to define a group of which a majority will commit further violence'.[34]

For the remainder of this discussion I shall make the currently optimistic assumption that the false positive rate is 50 per cent. This means that in imposing protective sentences, half the offenders are detained much longer than is necessary as they would not commit future serious violent crimes on earlier release. On the other hand, if there were no protective sentences, then half of those in the relevant group would commit violent crimes. Since a protective sentence is imposed solely for the purpose of preventing an offender from committing a future offence, and other offenders who have committed similar offences but are not judged to be dangerous get lighter sentences, it can be said that there is an injustice done to the 50 per cent of offenders who would not in fact have committed violent crimes had they been released earlier. Let us call these people 'unlucky offenders', and we shall assume that one 'unlucky offender' is detained to protect one innocent victim from a violent crime that would have been committed by another offender who is also under protective detention. So two offenders, only one of whom is an 'unlucky offender', are made to suffer for the benefit of one potential victim.

From the utilitarian point of view, in order to justify the protective sentence, one has to weigh the harm done to the two offenders against the harm to the potential victim. Given that the harm done to the victim of a serious crime—for example, being killed, brutally assaulted, or raped—is great, it would appear that the protective sentence is justified if the

[32] *Dangerousness and Criminal Justice*, pp. 31, 58.
[33] Nigel Walker, *Punishment, Danger and Stigma* (Oxford, 1980), p. 97.
[34] 'Unscientific, Unwise, Unprofitable or Unjust?', p. 277. See also *Punishment, Danger and Stigma*, p. 98; and Mark H. Moore, Susan R. Estrich, Daniel McGillis and William Spelman, *Dangerous Offenders: The Elusive Target of Justice*.

sentences imposed on the two offenders are not very long. But where the sentences are indeterminately long, as life sentences would be, it is unclear whether there is even a utilitarian justification unless the number of potential victims increases. However, the utilitarian approach does not exhaust the relevant considerations. We have a problem of distributive justice here, or, as the Floud Report rightly points out, there is the problem of 'effecting a just distribution of certain risks of grave harm: the grave harm that potentially recidivist offenders may do to their unknown victims and the grave harm which is suffered by offenders if they are subjected to the hardship of preventive measures which risk being unnecessary because they depend on predictive judgements of their conduct which are inherently uncertain'.[35] The Floud Report contains some illuminating discussion of when the risks of grave harm may be shifted from the victims to offenders. The Report has been subjected to close and helpful critical scrutiny, and I shall not attempt to review it here.[36] Instead I shall focus more generally on the types of considerations which seem to me to be morally relevant in arriving at an answer to the question as to whether protective sentencing is justified under the conditions specified so far.

We can divide the discussion into two stages, with the second stage incorporating considerations available in the first stage but also introducing new considerations. At the first stage, we consider the relative risks and harms to 'unlucky offenders' as opposed to those of the potential victims of crime. All offenders subjected to protective sentencing are certain of undergoing the suffering of being detained for a long period. Each offender also runs a 50 per cent risk of being an 'unlucky offender' whose punishment could have been avoided if we had enough knowledge. As against this, if there were no protective sentencing, then there would certainly be additional victims of serious crime, but the risk of any particular person becoming such a victim is not very high. Of course the risks

---

[35] *Dangerousness and Criminal Justice*, p. xvii.
[36] See Ted Honderich, 'On Justifying Protective Punishment'; A. E. Bottoms and Roger Brownsword, 'The Dangerousness Debate after the Floud Report'; and Nicola Lacey, 'Dangerousness and Criminal Justice: The Justification of Preventive Detention', *Current Legal Problems* (1983).

will not be the same for all since it depends on people's circumstances. Another relevant factor is that if a protective sentence is an extension of the punishment which the offender will in any case receive, then it carries with it the expression of society's moral disapproval which is an intrinsic feature of punishment. This is an additional harm to the 'unlucky offender' which has no analogue in the case of the harm inflicted on the victim of crime, except perhaps in the case of rape where the victim is sometimes unjustly stigmatized. However, this additional harm can be reduced if, as suggested by van den Haag, we adopt the 'dual track' system of the West German penal code which distinguishes between the offender's punishment according to desert for the crime already committed, and the subsequent non-punitive confinement if he is judged to be still dangerous.[37] If our resources permit, we can and should make the life of the person subjected to protective confinement as comfortable as is consistent with the purpose of the confinement. We can, for example, try to make his life no less tolerable than that of a disease carrier who is quarantined. But it is doubtful whether we will thereby make his protective sentence completely non-punitive in the way that quarantine is non-punitive.[38] The difficulty is that, unlike the person who is quarantined, he lives under the shadow of the offence that he has already committed which is the moral basis for his punishment, and also unavoidably part of the basis for his allegedly non-punitive protective sentence. The protective sentence is so closely linked with the past offence which is said to deserve punishment, and with the avoidance of a future culpable act, that it is difficult to view the sentence as something completely different from punishment.

So at the first stage, unless the protective sentence is relatively short, or the harm to potential victims especially grave, the relevant considerations lean towards the conclusion that protective sentencing is unjustified. The harms and risks endured by 'unlucky offenders' are greater than those of each potential victim, and on top of these there is the harm to other

[37] Ernest van den Haag, *Punishing Criminals* (New York, 1975), pp. 243–4. See also Nigel Walker, *Punishment, Danger and Stigma*, pp. 103–4.

[38] van den Haag himself acknowledges that the punitive effect of protective sentencing can be minimized but not removed altogether. See *Punishing Criminals*, p. 244.

offenders who are also detained. It is only when we move to the second stage that the picture changes significantly.

At the second stage, we introduce the feature of choice in the taking of risks, or control over one's actions, as morally relevant. When protective sentencing applies to those who have committed at least two serious offences, then any person who commits the first offence can be reminded of the existence of such protective sentencing. So the risk of being an 'unlucky offender' is one that he may choose to avoid. On the other hand, the victim of crime cannot avoid the risk of being harmed by criminal activity by taking reasonable precautions. This difference supports protective detention. The situation is such that whatever is done, that is whether or not protective sentencing is imposed, somebody will suffer. The alternative is that, on the one hand, 'unlucky offenders', who were aware of the sentence and had a fair opportunity to avoid it, are harmed, or, on the other hand, that law-abiding citizens, who had no such opportunity, are harmed as victims of serious crime. It does not seem unfair to distribute the risks of harm in favour of law-abiding citizens. Moreover, as I shall argue in the next chapter, the notion of desert does not dictate a specific punishment for a particular offence, but merely limits the range of permissible punishments. Hence so long as dangerous offenders are not punished beyond the limits applicable to their respective offences, they are not unjustly treated from the retributive point of view. So their punishment is compatible with, but not dictated by, retributive considerations.[39] The effect of a general reduction of sentences for serious offenders is that non-dangerous serious offenders will be punished below the upper limits for their respective offences, while dangerous serious offenders will be punished up to those limits.

The feature of choice or control helps to morally distinguish protective sentencing, applied to those who have already

[39] This basis for connecting the punishment of dangerous offenders with retributivism is different to that provided by the authors of *Dangerous Offenders: The Elusive Target of Justice*, pp. 55–61. They try to operate with a retributive notion of dangerous offenders which bases the offenders' punishment on their past criminal activities which show that they are 'the guiltiest offenders'. The punishment is therefore for their blameworthiness, and not because of predictions about their future conduct. But this overlooks the fact that if, for example, an offender's past criminal record, though very bad, somehow guarantees that he will not re-offend in future, then the problem of dangerousness will not arise.

committed serious offences, from the civil preventive detention
of allegedly dangerous persons before they commit any serious
crime. The absence of choice in the case of civil preventive
detention is a reason why, other things being equal, such
detention is more difficult to justify than the kind of protective
sentencing under consideration.[40]

I have discussed protective sentencing without focusing on
mentally ill offenders. However, when mental illness mitigates
an offence, the commission of the offence will lack some of
the features of genuine choice and control. In that case the
considerations at the first stage may well be decisive unless
the predictions of dangerousness rise above the 50 per cent
accuracy rate which has been assumed, or it is shown that the
harm that mentally ill offenders will cause is greater than the
harm that other dangerous offenders will cause. Similar considerations apply to those dangerous offenders, who are not
ill, in whom the notion of having control over their actions holds
good to a limited degree only.

But I have not erected a barrier of moral principle against
the protective sentencing of mentally ill offenders, or of others
who commit serious offences, if the predictions of dangerousness have a greater degree of accuracy. There is of course also
the problem of defining the notion of dangerousness in a
sufficiently tight and narrow manner so that a policy of protective sentencing cannot be easily abused. This involves a
definition of the grave or serious harm that dangerous offenders
are likely to commit. The Floud Report defined grave harm
as 'death; serious bodily injury; serious sexual assault; severe
or prolonged pain or mental stress; loss of or damage to property which causes severe personal hardship; damage to the
environment which has a severely adverse effect on public
health or safety; serious damage to the security of the State'.[41]
This is a start, but the definition does seem too broad.

[40] For two different views on the legitimacy of preventive detention, see: Andrew
von Hirsch, 'Prediction of Criminal Conduct and Preventive Confinement of Convicted Persons', and Ferdinand D. Schoeman, 'On Incapacitating the Dangerous',
both in Hyman Gross and Andrew von Hirsch (eds), *Sentencing* (New York, 1981).
[41] *Dangerousness and Criminal Justice*, p. 154.

THE AMOUNT OF PUNISHMENT

7.1. *Reducing Crime*

WHAT principles determine the extent or amount of punishment to be meted out to particular offenders? We shall begin by examining how the amount of punishment is arrived at from the utilitarian point of view, and then proceed in the next section to discuss retributive principles for fitting punishment to the crime.

It is widely accepted that, other things being equal, offenders who deliberately inflict greater harm on their victims should be punished more severely than those who inflict lesser harm. Thus the murderer should receive a much harsher punishment than the petty thief. But critics of utilitarianism sometimes claim that it cannot give a satisfactory account here because under appropriate circumstances the utilitarian has to condone severe punishment for minor offences. For example, K. G. Armstrong argues that if the death penalty were applied to a parking offence it would deter potential offenders, and so utilitarians who believe that the justification of punishment lies in its deterrent effect are committed to accepting the penalty. Again he maintains that if the reform of the criminal is what justifies punishment, then a person stealing a loaf of bread may have to be punished for the rest of his or her life if that is required for reformative purposes.[1]

Put so simply, the objections to the utilitarian theory of punishment for its alleged failure to observe a proportion between crime and punishment are not very persuasive. Utilitarians do not believe that any punishment which deters or rehabilitates offenders is justified irrespective of the nature of the offences. If indeed the only way to reform an offender

---

[1] K. G. Armstrong, 'The Retributivist Hits Back', in H. B. Acton (ed.), *The Philosophy of Punishment* (London, 1969), p. 152. See also C. W. K. Mundle, 'Punishment and Desert', in the same collection, p. 80. However, in the postscript to the paper Mundle has second thoughts. See p. 82.

who steals a loaf of bread is to subject him to a prolonged period of treatment, then it is obvious that the 'cure' is worse than the 'illness', and would for that reason alone be rejected. The utilitarian, who regards punishment as something that is in itself bad, will only justify a particular punishment if the suffering inflicted by that punishment is less than the harm caused by the crime which would have occurred had there been no punishment. And where several forms of punishment will achieve the same result, the utilitarian will accept the most lenient punishment because that minimizes suffering or unpleasantness. Thus if both capital punishment and some lesser punishment of imprisonment for a few years will be equally effective in deterring murder, then capital punishment is unjustified.

The utilitarian would not undergo a major operation, with many risks and possible complications, even if that were the only way in which he or she could be rid of an irritating itch which only recurred once in a long while. Similarly, the harm done by an offender who occasionally steals a loaf of bread is less than the suffering of the offender if he is imprisoned for many years to ensure that he never steals again. So it is better from the utilitarian point of view to tolerate the petty thefts and to avoid the harsh punishment if that is the only way to stop petty thefts. There is of course a difference between the case of the major operation and that of the severe punishment. In the former case, the benefits and harms to be weighed up are those of one and the same person. But in the case of the severe punishment, the failure to inflict it on the petty thief will result in someone else, namely the baker and possibly others, being inconvenienced by the loss of bread. But as far as the utilitarian is concerned, one has to weigh up impartially the suffering of the petty thief caused by the severe punishment against the nuisance to the baker caused by the loss of the loaves of bread. Given that the former is worse than the latter, it does not matter that the experiences are those of one and the same person or of two different persons.

Similar considerations will also rule out the death penalty for parking offences, effective as it undoubtedly would be. As Stanley Benn points out, the aim of the utilitarian is 'to select the penalty at which the aggregate of suffering caused by crimes actually committed and punishments actually inflicted would be the smallest possible'.[2] Benn goes on to argue that this provides the utilitarian with a basis for restricting severe penalties to serious offences if a serious offence is one which causes a great deal of suffering. 'If we call parking offences trivial, we mean that each one causes relatively little suffering; therefore, we are prepared to put up with a large number of them rather than incur the cost of making offenders suffer heavy penalties. Blackmail, on the other hand, causes so much suffering that if heavier penalties would yield even a small reduction in the number of offences, there might be a net gain even though offenders would suffer more than they did before.'[3] In his classic exposition of utilitarianism in *An Introduction to the Principles of Morals and Legislation,* Jeremy Bentham discusses 'the proportion between punishments and offences', and offers the following as one of the rules to be observed: '*The greater the mischief of the offence, the greater is the expense, which it may be worthwhile to be at, in the way of punishment.*'[4] So it looks as if the utilitarian can successfully meet the challenge of explaining why serious offences are punished more severely than minor offences. The more serious an offence, the greater the harm or suffering it causes, and hence the more severe the punishment may be before the suffering caused by punishment begins to outweigh the suffering caused by the offence.

But we have already seen in Chapter 2 how the aggregative nature of utilitarianism can result in the infliction of excessive punishment, and this suggests that the objection to the utilitarian that he or she would sanction a very severe exemplary punishment for a minor offence may still be correct if it is stated more carefully. So we shall try again with a different example. Suppose now that petty thefts are rife in a society and literally hundreds of cases occur weekly, and the thiefs are so efficient that it is rare for one to be caught. Although the harm caused by each theft is small, the total harm caused

[2] Stanley I. Benn, 'Punishment', in Jeffrie G. Murphy (ed.), *Punishment and Rehabilitation* (Belmont, 1973), p. 26. See also Ted Honderich, *Punishment, the Supposed Justifications* (Harmondsworth, 1984), pp. 58–60; and H. L. A. Hart, *Punishment and Responsibility* (Oxford, 1968), pp. 75–6, 163.

[3] 'Punishment' p. 27.

[4] Jeremy Bentham, *An Introduction to the Principles of Morals and Legislation* (eds) J. H. Burns and H. L. A. Hart (London & New York, 1982), p. 168.

by all the thefts is, from the utilitarian point of view, great, and may well outweigh the harm caused by the severe punishment of one petty thief. Suppose that in such a situation the application of a newly enacted law imposing a punishment of 10 years' imprisonment on a convicted petty thief, and the threat of repeating the penalty on future offenders will be sufficient to deter all other thiefs, and no lesser penalty will have any deterrent effect. It is arguable that the utilitarian would have to condone the imposition of 10 years' imprisonment on the one unfortunate petty thief who was unlucky enough to be caught.

There are of course all sorts of other considerations that a utilitarian who wishes to resist this conclusion will invoke—for example, the apprehension of the friends and relatives of petty thiefs that their loved ones will be the next victims of the draconian law. But it can be assumed that no such apprehension will be caused because people are reliably assured that the fear of the harsh penalty is so great that no one will ever again steal. In any case, such apprehension does not in itself capture the major objection to the punishment which is the injustice done to the offender in using him in this way for the benefit of society. The example shows that if we were guided solely by utilitarian considerations, then we would in some cases be much more willing to contemplate very severe exemplary punishments which are completely out of proportion to the actual harm caused by the particular offenders punished, as opposed to the total harm caused by similar offenders. Thus the injustice of the severe punishment for petty theft would be particularly acute if it were inflicted on a first offender because persistent offenders, who were the main targets of the exemplary punishment, could not be easily caught. So in real life it is not just the uncertainty about the effects of punishment, but also, and more importantly, the unfairness to the individuals punished, which make us set a limit to the severity of exemplary punishments. In expounding the sentencing policy of the English Court of Appeal Criminal Division, D. A. Thomas points out that the sentencer may ignore mitigating factors in order to promote general deterrence or other penal aims. But he also shows that 'these considerations are not normally held to justify a sentence which is disproportionate to the immediate offence'.[5] This limit on the severity of exemplary punishments is commendably non-utilitarian.

But it would be wrong to give the impression that the utilitarian theory would only commit us to use or to seriously consider the occasional use of very severe punishment for relatively minor offences. The disproportion between crime and punishment may also proceed along the opposite direction when very light penalties are imposed for very serious offences. Suppose that a certain kind of murder, for example the deliberate killing of a wife by a husband for financial gain, is rare and easily detectable. A small fine, with the attendant publicity and the forfeiture of all financial gain obtained, will be a sufficient individual and general deterrent. In that case, if the effects of the punishment are isolated to just this kind of murder, it would be appropriate on utilitarian grounds to punish the offence with a mere fine even though other kinds of murder are punished severely, and the other lesser offences still carry penalties of imprisonment.

One might try to extract from a suggestion of Bentham's another basis for punishing serious offences more severely than minor offences. He argued that we should induce a person to commit the lesser offence rather than the more serious offence by adopting the following rule: 'Where two offences come in competition, the punishment for the greater offence must be sufficient to induce a man to prefer the less.'[6] But it is in fact impossible to get more mileage out of this rule than its application to the very limited context for which it was perhaps intended. For example, if an offender, in making his escape, is confronted with the choice of injuring a person or killing him, then he would have no incentive to commit the lesser offence if this carried the heavier penalty. But for most offenders, not all offences are in Bentham's sense 'in competition' with one another. For example, the petty thief is not someone who is also a potential rapist, assailant, or murderer, who chooses to steal rather than to commit the more serious offence because of the harsher penalties for the latter offences. Rational investors will pick their way through various opportunities on a cost-benefit

---

[5] D. A. Thomas *Principles of Sentencing*, Second edn., (London, 1982), p. 47.
[6] *Principles of Morals and Legislation*, p. 168.

analysis. But is very doubtful that there are many offenders who survey the whole gamut of crimes and punishments, and then choose one rather than the others in terms of the relative leniency of its punishment.

The upshot of our discussion so far is that, although there are utilitarian arguments which would often be sufficient to justify imposing harsher punishment for more serious offences, these arguments are inadequate to account for both the strength of the commitment to the maintenance of a proportion between crime and punishment, and the great reluctance to depart occasionally from that proportion when required to do so by purely aggregative consequentialist considerations.

I have so far discussed the idea of having a proportion between crime and punishment in terms of the harm done by the crime. But the widely accepted view that punishment should be proportionate to the seriousness of the crime treats the seriousness of a crime not just in terms of the degree of harm caused, but also in terms of the culpability of the offender as indicated by his mental state when he committed the crime. Thus intentionally killing someone is treated as a more serious offence than negligently causing a person's death, even though in both cases the harm done is the same. This dimension of the proportionality between crime and punishment is something with which utilitarians have even greater difficulty in coming to terms. In Chapter 5 I have already argued for a non-utilitarian rationale of legal excuses. I shall now consider the extent to which it is possible to give a satisfactory utilitarian account of some of the factors that are generally recognized as mitigations, reducing but not eliminating the punishment for an offence.

However in sentencing policy the term 'mitigation' covers a broad range of very different considerations, each one reducing the sentence imposed.[7] Many of these have nothing to do with the character of the offence or with the circumstances under which the offence was committed. For example, sentencers sometimes reduce a sentence because of the undesirable effect that a long sentence will have on innocent dependants of the offender, or because of the ill health or advanced

---

[7] See D. A. Thomas, *Principles of Sentencing*, Ch. 4.

age of the offender.[8] The utilitarian will probably account for most of these mitigating factors on the ground that subjecting these offenders to the same amount of punishment as other offenders, who are more favourably placed, will cause an unnecessary increase in suffering. However, these factors do not affect the culpability of the offender and are not the type of mitigating factors which I have in mind. I shall restrict my discussion to two central mitigations, temptation and provocation, which reduces the offender's culpability. A poor man who steals because he is hungry acts under temptation. A man who assaults another who repeatedly verbally abuses him is provoked.

An often cited utilitarian reason for accepting temptation and provocation as mitigations is that more severe punishment would be unnecessary since the occasions on which people are subjected to temptations and provocations are few.[9] For example, a person who assaults only when provoked is unlikely to assault again since in the normal course of events he will not be provoked again. The reduced punishment meted out to him will also not have an adverse effect on general deterrence because normally an assailant cannot plead a similar mitigation. But the assumption that temptations and provocations seldom occur cannot be realistically generalized. For example, there are many occasions in domestic and personal relationships when strong passions are aroused by various provocations. Again, some members of minority racial groups are often subjected to provocative racialist taunts and harassments. But from the utilitarian point of view, given the undesirability of violent reactions to provocations, the amount of punishment to be inflicted depends on whether under the circumstances those provoked still have the capacity to abstain from harmful acts. If, as we are now assuming to be the case, offenders are capable of resisting the temptation or provocation, then punishment would be appropriate, and from the utilitarian point of view, if a lesser punishment is insufficient to prevent the criminal act, then more severe punishment may

[8] Ibid., Ch. 4. See also Hyman Gross, *A Theory of Criminal Justice* (New York, 1979), pp. 448–52.
[9] See the useful discussion in Ted Honderich, *Punishment, The Supposed Justifications*, pp. 68–71; and Stanley I. Benn, 'Punishment', pp. 30–1.

be justified. So the presence of temptations and provocations, instead of providing mitigations, may lead the utilitarian to increase the amount of punishment. Bentham recognized this when he wrote: 'The strength of the temptation, *caeteris paribus*, is as the profit of the offence: the quantum of the punishment must rise with the profit of the offence: *caeteris paribus*, it must therefore rise with the strength of the temptation. This there is no disputing.'[10] Bentham, however, struggled a little here because he also believed that the stronger the temptation the less certain we can be that the offender's act is evidence of his depravity. So he also recognized that the presence of temptation provided a basis for reducing the punishment because it did not reflect so badly on the offender's character. But for the utilitarian, the linkage between punishment and the character or blameworthiness of the offender can only be made if it is established that less punishment for those who are less bad or blameworthy will promote utilitarian ends. In many situations neither general nor individual deterrence is best achieved by the recognition of temptation and provocation as mitigations, and it is doubtful whether any other important utilitarian aim will be served.

Hart maintains that if, as he believes, the General Justifying Aim of punishment is a utilitarian one, then this will impose certain restrictions on the amount of punishment that may properly be inflicted. Thus punishments which result in more suffering than that caused by the offence unchecked will be disallowed. Again, a crime which causes greater suffering than another may be checked, if necessary, by a heavier penalty. But no greater penalty is justified if a lesser one will produce the same beneficial effects. However, Hart rightly points out that in addition to the restrictions dictated by the General Justifying Aim, there are also special limitations on the severity of punishment imposed by the idea of Mitigation, and these are independent of the General Justifying Aim of punishment. 'The special features of Mitigation are that a good reason for administering a less severe penalty is made out if the situation or mental state of the convicted criminal is such that he was exposed to an unusual or specially great temptation, or his

---

[10] *An Introduction to the Principle of Morals and Legislation*, p. 167.

ability to control his actions is thought to have been impaired or weakened otherwise than by his own action, so that conformity to the law which he has broken was a matter of special difficulty for him as compared with normal persons normally placed.'[11]

We can perhaps develop Hart's comment by saying that if, through no fault of his own, a person is confronted with a situation which made it very difficult for him to exercise self-control in conforming to the law, then he should receive a reduced sentence for his offence. It is not necessary that the situation be unusual, though it is important that the temptation or provocation is substantial. An example in which the provocation is generally accepted as being gross is that of a person who returns home unexpectedly and finds his or her spouse in bed with another person. But it would be relevant to ask whether the accused had contributed to the situation through constant cruelty and neglect.

The requirement that there be both absence of fault and loss of self-control is clearly met only in the central cases of provocation. In other cases that requirement may have to be relaxed a bit. Suppose, for example, a wife has endured for a long period the drunken violence of her husband who frequently beats her up. One day she buys a gun and kills him even though at the time of the killing he was neither drunk nor violent. It is very doubtful that her action can be described as impulsive, or that she was 'temporarily insane', though no doubt there will be those eager to maintain one or both of these fictions in order that she may avoid the full force of a murder charge. None the less there was a mitigation, and it would not be incorrect to say that she was severely provoked by her husband's conduct.

Andrew Ashworth suggests perceptively that the mitigating effect of provocation stems partly from the impulsivity or loss of self-control of the offender's act, and partly from the partial justification for the offender's response.[12] The partial justification applies when the offender's act can be viewed as an understandable response to the wrong done to him or her, and

---

[11] H. L. A. Hart, *Punishment and Responsibility*, p. 15.
[12] Andrew Ashworth, *Sentencing and Penal Policy* (London, 1983), p. 200. See also his helpful discussion on pp. 167–71, 176–7.

in that case as Ashworth points out, 'the enormity of that
wrong will largely determine the strength of the provocation'.[13]
Applying this to the above example, we cannot doubt the
enormity of the wrong done to the wife by the husband, and
this provides the basis for acknowledging the presence of strong
provocation. But it would appear that Ashworth himself would
not regard the type of case described as one of provocation.
He writes: 'It is the elements of suddenness and impulsivity
which serve to distinguish provocation as a mitigating factor
from revenge, which may be treated as an aggravating factor
because it is usually accompanied by planning and premedi-
tation.'[14] Certainly the elements of 'suddenness and impulsivity' are missing in our example. But the absence of these
elements, while sufficient to remove the example from the
central cases of provocation, is still insufficient to rule it out
as a case of provocation which is linked to the central cases
in various ways. Thus many people, subjected to the kind of
treatment endured for so long by the offender, would have lost
their self-control and reacted violently and impulsively much
earlier. In these other cases the mitigation of provocation
would undoubtedly apply. What differentiates our example
from these cases is the relative passivity or tolerance, or the
greater fear, of the offender. In so far as we are inclined to
refer to provoking situations as those apt to cause certain kinds
of reactions in normal people, we are prepared to speak of
provocation as present when the external circumstances are
the same, but the particular reaction differs to some extent.

No doubt much more can be said about other non-central
cases where the mitigating effects of provocation should also
be acknowledged. But we already have enough to show that
the idea of mitigation is much more closely linked to notions
of reduced blameworthiness and loss of self-control than it is
to any forward-looking aim of reducing crime.

7.2. *Just Deserts*

Retributivists base the amount of punishment that an offender
should receive on his just desert. Various principles are used

---

[13] Ibid., p. 168.
[14] Ibid., p. 169.

for determining the offender's desert, some of which seek to arrive at a specific punishment while others settle for an ordinal scale in which the appropriate punishment for an offence is based on the relative moral gravity of the offence when compared with other offences.

Many of those who support capital punishment for murder invoke the *lex talionis*: an eye for an eye, a tooth for a tooth, and a life for a life. Apart from the occasional demand, and the practice in some countries, that the assailant should be flogged, capital punishment seems to be the only form of punishment which is still frequently supported by appeals to the *lex talionis*. The *lex talionis* attempts to provide a simple basis for arriving at a specific punishment for each crime, and the principle embodied in it is that the punishment should inflict on the offender what he has done to his victim.

The defects of the *lex talionis* are obvious and fundamental. It cannot be applied to many crimes, and even when it is applicable the formula for its application is too crude and sometimes requires forms of punishment which are morally unacceptable.

An indication of the very wide range of offences to which the *lex talionis* has no application is given in this catalogue by Kleinig: 'what penalty would you inflict on a rapist, a blackmailer, a forger, a dope peddler, a multiple murderer, a smuggler, or a toothless fiend who has knocked somebody else's teeth out?'[15] Indeed it would appear that the single murder is one of the few cases in which the *lex talionis* can be applied literally.

But even in the case of murder the weaknesses of the *lex talionis* are evident. It depends on a description of the crime which is crude and general—one eye is just like any other eye, and one life like another. But when one specifies in greater detail the eye or the tooth or the life that has been lost through criminal actions, it may not be possible to do to the offender what he has done to his victim. The offender may not have as good an eye or tooth as his victim's to be taken away. And in the case of murder. Blackstone has remarked: 'the

[15] John Kleinig, *Punishment and Desert* (The Hague, 1973), p. 120. Kleinig's discussion of the *lex talionis* on pp. 120–3 is very useful, and the rest of Ch. VII also contains interesting points relevant to some of the issues raised in this section.

execution of a needy decrepit assassin is a poor satisfaction for the murder of a nobleman in the bloom of his youth, and full enjoyment of his friends, his honours, and his fortune'.[16]

An even more important objection to the *lex talionis* is that the formula it uses for determining the correct punishment is solely in terms of the harm done by the crime, and makes no allowance for the morally important mental states of the offender, or for the mitigating or aggravating circumstances of the crime.[17] A person's death can be brought about deliberately, recklessly, negligently, or accidentally. A strict application of the *lex talionis* involves the imposition of the death penalty in all these cases. This will mean an extension of the death penalty to cover cases ranging from the most sadistic murder, to acts of mercy killing and to deaths caused accidentally. On the other hand, it is not clear how that formula can be modified to allow the punishment to reflect the appropriate mental state of the offender. How does one arrange for the offender who kills to be executed recklessly, negligently, or accidentally? And how does one punish the offender who deliberately shoots to kill but only fails because he was a bad shot, or because of the chance intervention of an object?

Finally, even if all these problems can be solved, we are still confronted with the moral constraint on certain forms of punishment which are too cruel to be tolerated by any civilized penal system. A sadistic murderer or assailant subjects his victim to the most horrible torture. Let us assume that he has recorded the whole episode on a video cassette for his own future enjoyment. It is therefore possible to punish him by inflicting on him all that he has done to his victim, blow by sadistic blow. But even if there are volunteers prepared to re-enact the torture with the offender as the victim, it would be barbarous to permit such punishment.[18]

The *lex talionis* is the oldest retributive formula for determining the amount of punishment. It has been said that historically

---

[16] Quoted by H. L. A. Hart, *Punishment and Responsibility*, p. 161.

[17] The point is well made by John Kleinig, *Punishment and Desert*, pp. 120–1.

[18] Jeffrey H. Reiman argues that although the death penalty for murder is a just punishment based on the *lex talionis*, the death penalty should none the less be abolished as part of 'the civilizing mission of modern states'. See his, 'Justice, Civilization, and the Death Penalty: Answering van den Haag', *Philosophy & Public Affairs*, 14 (1985).

the *lex talionis* was used not to demand retribution but to set a limit to it.[19] It prevents the exaction of excessive penalties when feelings of vengeance are on the loose.

It is tempting to think that the *lex talionis* is only one particular interpretation of a more general retributive principle which is capable of other, and more plausible, interpretations. The more general principle is that the punishment and the crime should be equal or equivalent. One way of ensuring the equality is to repeat what the offender has done with the roles reversed. But just as one can repay the borrowed sugar by returning something else deemed to be of equal value, so too it might be thought that punishment gives offenders their just deserts if it inflicts on them the degree of suffering which is judged to be equivalent to the suffering caused by their respective crimes. Interpreted in this manner, the principle resembles the utilitarian doctrine in some respects in that it reduces both the crime and the punishment to a common denominator, the suffering caused, against which they may be compared. But it differs from utilitarianism in insisting that the punishment must equal the crime irrespective of the consequences produced by such equality. So even when a lesser punishment will serve to reduce crime more effectively than a greater punishment, the latter is still be to be meted out if it is the deserved or equivalent punishment. Moreover, the equality or equivalence between crime and punishment restricts the relevant suffering to, on the one hand, that inflicted on the victim or victims of crime, and, on the other hand, the suffering of the offender as a result of the punishment. Without these restrictions, the equivalence between crime and punishment will depend on too many factors that are not within the offender's control and are only incidentally connected with the crime. For example, non-victims may be shocked by the news of a crime in the neighbourhood, and their shock may in turn affect the lives of others close to them.

It is of course unclear how one could arrive at a specific punishment which is, in the sense required, the equivalent of the offence. But even if this objection is waived, we have not

---

[19] Ernest van den Haag, *Punishing Criminals* (New York, 1975), p. 193 n. See also John Kleinig, *Punishment and Desert*, p. 121.

got round all the objections raised against the *lex talionis*. The notion of 'equivalent' or 'equal' punishment must be a moral notion if it is to justify the punishment. We saw earlier that the prolonged torture of a sadistic murderer or assailant is morally unacceptable as a form of punishment. But the moral objection to torture would presumably apply to any other form of punishment which is regarded as the moral equivalent of torture. Again, like the *lex talionis*, the principle that crime and punishment should be equivalent focuses on the harm or suffering caused by the crime, and ignores the mental state of the offender. But any attempt to remedy the principle by taking account of the offender's culpability will only destroy the principle. For now the common denominator of suffering caused is not the only relevant consideration. Suffering caused by deliberate acts calls for greater punishment than the same suffering caused by merely negligent acts. But how is one to combine the suffering caused by a crime with the appropriate mental state to yield an equivalent punishment? Punishment is deliberately inflicted suffering, and how is it to be equated with a certain amount of suffering that is not caused deliberately but recklessly or negligently?

Most contemporary retributivists settle for the proportionality principle that the amount of punishment should be proportionate to the moral seriousness or moral gravity of offences, with the more serious offences being punished more severely than the less serious. This principle provides a particular interpretation of the more general idea that there should be a proportion between crime and punishment.[20] (We saw earlier how Bentham tried to give a utilitarian account of the general idea.) The application of the proportionality principle involves constructing two ordinal scales, one of punishments and the other of crimes. Punishments are ranked in order of severity, and crimes are ranked in order of moral seriousness. The most severe punishment on the scale is reserved for the most serious offence, the next most severe punishment for the second most serious offence, and so on. In general the ranking of punishments in order of severity is easy compared with the assessment of the relative moral gravity of offences.

[20] See H. L. A. Hart, *Punishment and Responsibility*, pp. 233–4.

According to the retributivist, the moral seriousness of an offence is a function of two major factors—the harm done by the offence and the culpability of the offender as indicated by his mental state at the time of committing the offence. Other things being equal, killing is more serious than assault, and intentional killing is more serious than negligently causing death. The interplay of these two factors, harm and culpability, is important, and it is often not possible to know the full significance of one factor without reference to the other factor. When told that a person has deliberately or recklessly caused harm, we do not know how serious the offence is unless we also know the extent of the harm. Ignoring the high probability of a very minor harm is not worse than ignoring a lesser probability of causing greater harm.

I suggested earlier that it is impossible to combine the harm and culpability features of an offence to yield a specific punishment which is the moral equivalent of the offence. But the construction of an ordinal scale of crimes is a project that seems capable of being carried out. Those who are sceptical should look at analogous cases. Thus when tutors and teachers rank the essays of their students, they do not have only one relevant feature to look for. There are a number of different features—originality, understanding of the issues discussed, lucidity of presentation, etc.—which each makes a contribution to the quality of the essay. An essay may be strong in one dimension but weak in another, and yet it is possible to make an overall assessment of the essay as being better or worse than another. Indeed it is also possible to argue that one essay is only marginally better than another essay, whereas it is considerably better than a third essay. Of course such judgements are sometimes controversial, but a teacher knows how to argue for his or her judgement by pointing to relevant features of the essays and the relative weights to be given to each feature in the context of the work as a whole. Now the problems faced by retributivists in ranking offences are not very different from those confronting teachers in ranking essays. The judgements about the relative moral seriousness of offences will also be controversial, and there will be detailed references to various aspects of offences. No one has done the job for the whole range of offences, although recently Andrew

Ashworth has made an excellent start with a detailed account of violent and property offences.[21]

I shall not attempt to summarize Ashworth's discussion, but two points of more general interest are worth commenting on. First, Ashworth rightly argues that in assessing the culpability of offenders, one has to break down the broad categories of mental attitudes constituting the *mens rea* required for criminal conduct.[22] The mental states of intention and recklessness can be present in various forms. Thus an offender can be said to have intended a harm both when he carefully planned and deliberated before causing the harm, and when he acted on the spur of the moment. But this difference is relevant to the moral evaluation of his conduct. There are similar morally relevant distinctions between types of recklessness. Ashworth suggests crimes involving planned recklessness may be more serious than those committed intentionally but impulsively.

The second general point is Ashworth's defence of what he calls the 'subjective principle of sentencing' which is that 'an offender should be sentenced on the basis of what he intended to do or knowingly risked doing'.[23] This has the implication that 'where a person intends only to commit an assault but his act unforeseeably causes death', he should be convicted only of assault, and, on the other hand, 'where an offender intended to inflict more harm than he succeeded in inflicting, he should be sentenced on the basis of what he tried to do'.[24] This principle links the offender's punishment to outcomes that he had chosen at least in the sense that he chose to risk those outcomes. It severs the link between punishment and

---

[21] Andrew Ashworth, *Sentencing and Penal Policy*, esp. Ch. 4. See also: Sir Rupert Cross and Andrew Ashworth, *The English Sentencing System*, Third edn. (London, 1981); Andrew von Hirsch, 'Doing Justice: The Principle of Commensurate Deserts', in Hyman Gross and Andrew von Hirsch (eds), *Sentencing* (New York & Oxford, 1981); Hugo Adam Bedau, 'Retribution and the Theory of Punishment', and Andrew von Hirsch, 'Proportionality and Desert: A Reply to Bedau', both in *The Journal of Philosophy*, 75 (1978).

[22] *Sentencing and Penal Policy*, pp. 150–3.

[23] Ibid., p. 154. See also Andrew Ashworth, 'Sharpening the Subjective Element in Criminal Liability', and John Harris, 'Over-exertion and Under-achievement', both in Anthony Duff and Nigel Simmonds (eds), *Philosophy and the Criminal Law* (Wiesbaden, 1984).

[24] Ibid., p. 154.

those outcomes which eventuated or failed to eventuate through pure chance.

Now retributivists ought to accept the view that a person's culpability for his or her actions should not be affected by chance events over which the agent had no control and could not reasonably have foreseen. But this view supports something broader than the subjective principle of sentencing, and extends criminal liability to harms that are the product of grossly negligent acts. As has been argued in Chapter 5, the harm caused by such actions are in the relevant sense within an agent's control in that he or she had the capacity and opportunity to prevent the occurrence of the harm by taking appropriate preventive action. To the extent that agents did not take the necessary reasonable precautions to avoid the harm, to that extent they are at fault and culpable even though they did not knowingly risk the harm. Ashworth himself acknowledges the case for criminal liability for negligent failure to attain statutory standards of safety in factories, but he does not relate this back to the subjective principle, and his discussion seems to give insufficient weight to the culpability for such negligence.[25] The question he poses is 'whether a negligent failure to attain statutory standards of safety ought to be ranked as morally worse or not so blameworthy as the deliberate stealing of, say, a bottle of whisky'.[26] He acknowledges that the maximum penalties for such negligence are relatively low, but suggests that instead of severer penalties for such offences perhaps 'more sparing prosecution and lower penalties for minor property offences would be a more appropriate solution'.[27] But the culpability for negligence can vary in degrees, and grossly negligent failure to meet important safety standards which protect the health and lives of employees can be a serious offence, quite unlike the deliberate stealing of a bottle of whisky. The implications of taking seriously some kinds of negligent conduct have already been considered in Chapter 5 in our discussion of the Morgan rape case.

I have suggested one direction in which the subjective principle should be extended. But there is also another way in

[25] Ibid., pp. 192–4.
[26] Ibid., p. 192.
[27] Ibid., p. 193.

which it should be contracted to prevent unnecessary prosecution and punishment. Suppose a man, who has a superstitious belief, tries to kill his enemy by sticking pins into his wax image.[28] It would not be necessary to punish him if it turns out that this is the only method by which he will attempt to kill his enemy, and that repeated failure to get the desired result will not lead him to switch to a reliable means. But on a strict application of the subjective principle of sentencing, a severe sentence would be in order. This suggests that the subjective principle is only acceptable when it is applied to cases in which there is harm or the likelihood of harm.

I have considered some of the issues raised by the application of the proportionality principle, and suggested that it is possible to rank crimes in order of their moral seriousness. One should now distinguish between a thin version of the proportionality principle and a thick version. The thin version is satisfied if one can construct purely ordinal scales of crime and punishment, and the serious offences are punished more relative to the less serious ones. The overall level of punishment, the amount of punishment for each offence, and the intervals between the punishments for adjacent offences on the ordinal scale are not considered. It is obvious that the thin proportionality principle on its own cannot determine the amount of punishment to be meted out to various offences. The requirement that punishment should vary with the relative moral seriousness of the offences can be met by too many scales of punishment imposing vastly different amounts of punishment for the same offence.

The thick version of the proportionality principle does not stop at the construction of ordinal scales, but also seeks to determine the extent of the differences in the punishment for various offences on the scale. The idea that punishment should be proportionate to the moral seriousness of the offence is now interpreted to include some version of the requirement that serious offences should be punished severely and minor offences leniently. This goes beyond the condition set by a

[28] For a discussion of this type of case, see H. L. A. Hart, 'The House of Lords on Attempting the Impossible', in his collection of *Essays in Jurisprudence and Philosophy* (Oxford, 1983), p. 389. See also: Jeremy Waldron, 'Critical Notice of Hart's *Essays in Jurisprudence and Philosophy*', *Mind*, 94 (1985), pp. 281–3; and John Harris, 'Overexertion and Under-achievement', p. 95.

relative scale of punishment which merely ensures that the punishment for the serious offences should be more than those for the less serious ones. As far as such a purely ordinal scale is concerned, all punishments can be severe or all lenient. On the other hand, the thick proportionality principle will insist that if one offence is only slightly more serious than another, then the difference in punishment should not be vast. But where two offences vary greatly in their seriousness, this difference should be reflected in the big difference between their respective punishments. While all thick versions of the proportionality principle will, in this manner, seek to regulate the intervals between punishments on the ordinal scales, one can have thicker and yet thicker versions, with the thickest version aiming at the greatest amount of fine tuning in the scales of punishment.

But the idea that a serious offence should be punished severely need not include the requirement that there should be a specific punishment which properly reflects the moral seriousness of the offence. For any attempt to arrive at such a punishment will take us back to the *lex talionis* or to the notion of an equivalence between crime and punishment. According to the thick proportionality principle, the basis for saying that the punishment for a certain offence is not sufficiently severe is that it does not reflect the moral gravity of the offence relative to those of other offences. In addition there will have to be some very general conception of what kinds of punishment are lenient and what kinds severe. But although the thick proportionality principle will exclude some scales of punishment which are consistent with the thin proportionality principle, it still leaves the issue of the desirable level of punishment fairly open. There are still several scales of punishment which will satisfy the thick proportionality principle, and the range of permissible punishments for each offence will be quite broad.

It is at this point that one can allow utilitarian considerations to operate within the requirements of the thick proportionality principle. The constraints imposed by the principle on the pursuit of utilitarian aims rule out the kinds of exemplary punishments considered earlier in which a minor offender received a very heavy penalty. They also rule out a small fine for certain types of murder even if this can be justified on purely utilitarian grounds. The thick proportionality principle lays down fairly broad limits of permissible punishments for each offence, and within those limits utilitarian considerations may operate freely in arriving at the punishment which will be most effective in reducing crime. It remains to be seen what guidelines to sentencing such a combination of retributive and utilitarian considerations can provide.

7.3. *Sentencing*

In recent years, indeterminate sentencing has come under heavy attack. Such sentencing is associated with the rehabilitation of offenders which is for some the main General Justifying Aim of punishment. Rehabilitation calls for the individualization of punishment to suit the particular needs of each offender, and although it does not require indeterminate sentencing, such sentencing was seen as providing the flexibility for the successful implementation of rehabilitative programmes. But it is now widely accepted that these programmes have largely failed, although it is possible that more modest claims for the limited success of some programmes can be sustained.[29] There have also been strong moral objections to those rehabilitative programmes which ignore the rights of offenders, and provide insufficient safeguards against the abuse of official power in depriving offenders of their liberty, welfare, and dignity.

Concern has also been expressed about the vast discretionary powers available to sentencers with the resulting disparities in the punishments imposed on similar offenders who have committed very similar offences. In America serious efforts have been made to remove such disparities. The suggested reforms have generally been directed by the revival of retributivism as the basis of sentencing.[30]

---

[29] See Robert Martinson, 'New Findings, New Views: A Note of Caution Regarding Sentencing Reform', *Hofstra Law Review*, 7 (1979). Martinson maintains that 'no treatment program now used in criminal justice is inherently either substantially helpful or harmful. The critical fact seems to be the conditions under which the program is delivered. For example, our results indicate that a widely-used program, such as formal education, is detrimental when given to juvenile sentenced offenders in a group home, but is beneficial (decreases reprocessing rates) when given to juveniles in juvenile prisons' (pp. 254–5).

[30] For a helpful exposition and critical assessment of recent trends in sentencing

There are of course numerous ways of removing or reducing disparities in sentences and the discretionary powers of judges in sentencing. The most extreme proposal is to allow the legislature to fix specific punishments for each type of offence, and the judge is only left to determine the category into which the offender falls. The judge may not vary the so-called 'flat-time' or determinate sentence, and he may not adjust sentences to take account of aggravating or mitigating factors. 'Presumptive sentences' also lay down specific punishments for each variant of a certain type of crime. Aggravating and mitigating factors are specified, and each such factor will increase or decrease the punishment specified by a fixed amount. The judge's duty in sentencing is to classify the offence according to the correct variant, and to determine whether aggravating or mitigating factors are present. It is of course possible to modify the system of sentencing to allow the judge discretion in exceptional cases to depart from the presumptive sentence. This modification will bring the system closer to what has been called the 'guidelines' approach to sentencing.

One 'guidelines' approach bases sentencing guidelines on the past sentencing practices of the courts. The guidelines specify a range of sentences for each type of offence, and the judge may only go outside the range set if he or she gives written reasons for the departure.

There can be many variations of the guidelines approach depending on the content of the guidelines. For example, retributivists, who reject the principles embodied in the actual practices of the courts, will wish to substitute some version of the proportionality principle as the basis of the guidelines. Nor is it the case that the guidelines can only be based on retributive considerations to the exclusion of all utilitarian considerations. The general value of the guidelines approach is that it reduces, without eliminating, the discretion of judges

reform, see D. J. Galligan, 'Guidelines and Just Deserts: A Critique of Recent Trends in Sentencing Reform', *The Criminal Law Review* (1981). See also, from the vast literature: Martin L. Forst (ed.), *Sentencing Reform: Experiments in Reducing Disparity* (Beverly Hills, 1982); Sir Rupert Cross and Andrew Ashworth, *The English Sentencing System* pp. 204–17; Hyman Gross and Andrew von Hirsch (eds), *Sentencing*, pp. 303–35; and Hugo Adam Bedau, 'Classification-Based Sentencing: Some Conceptual and Ethical Issues', in J. R. Pennock and J. Chapman (eds), *Nomos XXVII: Criminal Justice* (New York, 1985).

and makes sentencing into a more principled enterprise. Its more specific value depends on the content of the guidelines.

It is possible to fit the combination of retributive and utilitarian considerations for determining the amount of punishment into the formal framework of the guidelines approach to sentencing. As indicated earlier, the range of penalties that is consistent with the thick proportionality principle is fairly broad. Utilitarian considerations are introduced to narrow the range of punishment that is appropriate for each type of offence, and to determine the general level and form of punishment. But the rankings of offences will be in accordance with the proportionality principle. The guidelines to the sentencing judge will reflect the narrower utilitarianly shaped ranges. The relevant utilitarian considerations are mainly those of general deterrence and incapacitation. Particular attention will have to be paid to when imprisonment as a form of punishment should be used, and to the duration of such imprisonment. These are issues to which I shall return shortly.

Once the guidelines have been established, the sentencer will almost invariably have to fix the appropriate punishment for a particular offender somewhere within the range of penalties for the relevant category of offence. In arriving at his or her decision the sentencer will take account of aggravations and mitigations, and state the reasons for the particular sentence. As Norval Morris points out, if judges routinely give their reasons for the sentences they impose, this will lead to principled sentencing.[31] If the range of penalties for an offence does not already include a suspended sentence or probation, then some discretion may be given to sentencers to hand down these sentences in exceptional circumstances where the mitigating factors are very great. Similarly, there may be exceptionally aggravating and unusual factors which warrant a sentence beyond the upper limit set by the guidelines. (This will rarely violate the proportionality principle because the range of punishments set by the guidelines is narrower than the range that is consistent with that principle.) If predictions of dangerousness become sufficiently reliable, then they may be incorporated into the guidelines which will provide for longer sentences for dangerous offenders.

[31] Norval Morris, *The Future of Imprisonment* (Chicago & London, 1974), p. 80.

Sherman and Hawkins point out that American penal policy and practice have for a long time been dominated by 'the fusion of punishment with prison'.[32] They maintain that there is an indiscriminate sentencing of various offenders to prison, and the time served in prison seems to be unrelated to the offence. They themselves see the primary aim of prison as that of incapacitating offenders, and suggest that imprisonment should be much more selectively used to incarcerate mainly those who commit violent crimes against the person. They also argue that long prison sentences are inefficient in reducing crime. 'With the peak offence rates for imprisonable crimes concentrated in the late teens and early twenties, the first year of a prison sentence prevents far more crimes than the tenth year.'[33] They therefore recommend the imprisonment for at least some time of all those who qualify, but suggest that the normal maximum duration of imprisonment should be five years.

We know that the prison population in many countries is rising. In the Western world, the overcrowding in prisons has not reached the proportions in Brazil where recently prisoners, desperate to draw attention to their plight, drew up a list among themselves of who were to be killed by other prisoners, and several prisoners were killed in this manner.[34] But our prisons too are overcrowded, and many of them are outdated. Part of the cause seems to lie in 'the fusion of punishment with prison' to which Sherman and Hawkins refer. Whether or not their specific proposals to break down this fusion are acceptable is one thing. But it cannot be doubted that punishment includes more than imprisonment, and our guidelines will have to consider a more discriminate use of imprisonment, and also the possibility that very long periods of imprisonment should only be rarely imposed. Justice and prudence may happily come together.

Crime will be with us, and punishment, whether it be draconian or soft, will not eliminate it. But we should seek, as best we can, to reduce crime without sacrificing fundamental

[32] Michael Sherman and Gordon Hawkins, *Imprisonment in America* (Chicago & London, 1981), p. 99.
[33] Ibid., p. 110.
[34] See *The Times* (5 June 1985).

moral values. Crimes and criminals are too various to be fitted into any one simple explanation. But each perceived increase in crime is likely to be met with demands for more and more severe punishment. We often claim that such punishment merely gives offenders what they deserve, but we have no coherent theory of deserts which justifies the claim. We also claim that severe punishment will deter criminals more, but we are often wrong, and are prompted not by respect for the facts, but by dark and dangerous passions. We have to accept that the fight against crime will not normally produce quick and dramatic results. But progress is possible.

BIBLIOGRAPHY

Acton, H. B. (ed.) *The Philosophy of Punishment* (London, 1969).

Andenaes, Johannes, 'Does Punishment Deter Crime?', in Ezorsky, G. (ed.), *Philosophical Perspectives on Punishment* (Albany, 1972), 342–57.

Anscombe, G. E. M., 'Does Oxford Moral Philosophy Corrupt Youth?', *The Listener* (14 February, 1957), 266–7, 271.

Armstrong, K. G., 'The Retributivist Hits Back', in Acton, H. B. (ed.), *The Philosophy of Punishment* (London, 1969), 138–58.

Arneson, Richard J., 'The Principle of Fairness and Free-Rider Problems', *Ethics*, 92 (1982), 616–33.

Ashworth, Andrew, *Sentencing and Penal Policy* (London, 1983).

—— 'Sharpening the Subjective Element in Criminal Liability', in Duff, Anthony and Simmonds, Nigel (eds), *Philosophy and the Criminal Law* (Wiesbaden, 1984), 79–89.

Austin, J. L., 'A Plea for Excuses', in Austin, J. L., *Philosophical Papers* (eds), J. O. Urmson and G. J. Warnock (Oxford, 1961), 123–52.

Bayles, Michael D., 'Character, Purpose, and Criminal Responsibility', *Law and Philosophy*, 1 (1982), 5–20.

Bedau, Hugo Adam, 'Retribution and the Theory of Punishment', *The Journal of Philosophy*, 75 (1978), 601–20.

—— 'Classification-Based Sentencing: Some Conceptual and Ethical Issues', in Pennock, J. R. and Chapman, J. (eds), *Nomos XXVII: Criminal Justice* (New York, 1985), 89–118.

Benn, Stanley I., 'Punishment', in Murphy, Jeffrie G. (ed.), *Punishment and Rehabilitation* (Belmont, 1973), 18–34.

Bentham, Jeremy, *An Introduction to the Principles of Morals and Legislation* (eds) J. H. Burns and H. L. A. Hart (London & New York, 1982).

Blumstein, Alfred, Cohen, Jacqueline, and Nagin, Daniel (eds), *Deterrence and Incapacitation: Estimating the Effects of Criminal Sanctions on Crime Rates*, National Academy of Sciences, Panel on Research on Deterrent and Incapacitative Effects (Washington, 1978).

Bottoms, A. E. and Brownsword, Roger, 'The Dangerousness Debate after the Floud Report', *British Journal of Criminology*, 22 (1982), 229–54.

Burgh, Richard W., 'Do the Guilty Deserve Punishment?', *The Journal of Philosophy*, 79 (1982), 193–210

Cederblom, J. B., and Bilzek, William L., *Justice and Punishment* (Cambridge, Massachusetts, 1976).

Cohen, Jacqueline, 'The Incapacitative Effect of Imprisonment: A Critical Review of the Literature', in Blumstein, A., Cohen, J., and Nagin, J. (eds.), *Deterrence and Incapacitation: Estimating the*

Effects of Criminal Sanctions on Crime Rates (Washington, 1978), 187–233.

Cooper, David E., 'Hegel's Theory of Punishment', in Pelcynski, Z. A. (ed.), *Hegel's Political Philosophy: Problems and Perspectives* (Cambridge, 1971), 151–67.

Cottingham, John, 'Varieties of Retribution', *The Philosophical Quarterly*, 29 (1979), 238–46.

Cross, Sir Rupert and Ashworth, Andrew, *The English Sentencing System*, Third edn. (London, 1981).

Curley, E. M., 'Excusing Rape', *Philosophy and Public Affairs*, 5 (1976), 325–60.

Davies, Lawrence H., 'They Deserve to Suffer', *Analysis*, 32 (1971–2), 136–40.

Dennett, Daniel C., *Elbow Room* (Oxford, 1984).

Duff, Anthony and Simmonds, Nigel (eds), *Philosophy and the Criminal Law* (Wiesbaden, 1984).

Dworkin, Ronald, *Taking Rights Seriously* (London, 1978).

Ezorsky, Gertrude, (ed.), *Philosophical Perspectives on Punishment* (Albany, 1972).

—— 'The Ethics of Punishment', in Ezorsky, Gertrude (ed.), *Philosophical Perspectives on Punishment* (Albany, 1972), xi–xxvii.

—— 'Punishment and Excuses', in Goldinger, Milton (ed.), *Punishment and Human Rights* (Cambridge, 1974), 99–115.

Feinberg, Joel, 'Crime, Clutchability, and Individuated Treatment', in Murphy, Jeffrie G. (ed.), *Punishment and Rehabilitation* (Belmont, 1973), 217–34.

—— 'The Expressive Function of Punishment', in Gross, Hyman and von Hirsch, Andrew (eds), *Sentencing* (New York & Oxford, 1981), 23–36.

Fingarette, Herbert, *The Meaning of Criminal Insanity* (Berkeley & Los Angeles, 1974).

Finnis, John, 'Old and New in Hart's Philosophy of Punishment', *The Oxford Review*, 8 (1968), 73–80.

—— 'The Restoration of Retribution', *Analysis*, 32 (1971–2), 131–5.

—— 'Meaning and Ambiguity in Punishment (and Penology)', *Osgooge Hall Law Journal*, 10 (1972), 264–8.

—— *Natural Law and Natural Rights* (Oxford, 1980).

—— *Fundamentals of Ethics* (Oxford, 1983).

Fletcher, George, *Rethinking Criminal Law* (Boston & Toronto, 1978).

Flew, Antony, 'The Justification of Punishment', in Acton, H. B. (ed.), *The Philosophy of Punishment* (London, 1969), 83–104.

Floud, Jean, 'Dangerousness and Criminal Justice', *British Journal of Criminology*, 22 (1982), 213–28.

Floud, Jean and Young, Warren, *Dangerousness and Criminal Justice* (London, 1981) (The Floud Report).

Forst, Martin L., (ed.), *Sentencing Reform: Experiments in Reducing Disparity* (Beverly Hills, 1982).

Fuller, Lon L., *The Morality of Law* (New Haven, 1964).

Galligan, D. J., 'Guidelines and Just Deserts: A Critique of Recent Trends in Sentencing Reform', *The Criminal Law Review* (1981), 297–311.

—— 'The Return to Retribution in Penal Theory', in Tapper, C. (ed.), *Crime, Proof and Punishment* (London, 1981), 144–71.

Gauthier, David P., *The Logic of Leviathan* (Oxford, 1969).

Gibbs, Jack P., *Crime, Punishment, and Deterrence* (New York, 1975).

Golding, Martin P., *Philosophy of Law* (Englewood Cliffs, 1975).

Goldinger, Milton, (ed.), *Punishment and Human Rights* (Cambridge, 1974).

Gross, Hyman, *A Theory of Criminal Justice* (New York, 1979).

Gross, Hyman, and von Hirsch, Andrew (eds), *Sentencing* (New York & Oxford, 1981).

Hampshire, Stuart, *Two Theories of Morality* (Oxford, 1977).

Hampton, Jean, 'The Moral Education Theory of Punishment', *Philosophy & Public Affairs*, 13 (1984), 208–38.

Hare, R. M. 'The Argument from Received Opinion', in Hare, R. M., *Essays on Philosophical Method* (London, 1971), 117–35.

—— *Moral Thinking: Its Levels, Method and Point* (Oxford, 1981).

Harris, John, 'Over-exertion and Under-achievement', in Duff, Anthony and Simmonds, Nigel (eds) *Philosophy and the Criminal Law* (Wiesbaden, 1984), 91–8.

Hart, H. L. A., 'Are There Any Natural Rights?' *Philosophical Review*, 64 (1955), 175–91.

—— *The Concept of Law* (Oxford, 1961).

—— *Punishment and Responsibility* (Oxford, 1968).

—— 'Introduction', in Bentham, Jeremy, *An Introduction to the Principles of Morals and Legislation* (eds), J. H. Burns and H. L. A. Hart (London & New York, 1982), xxxiii–ixx.

—— 'Between Utility and Rights', in Hart, H. L. A., *Essays in Jurisprudence and Philosophy* (Oxford, 1983), 198–222.

—— 'The House of Lords on Attempting the Impossible', in Hart, H. L. A., *Essays in Jurisprudence and Philosophy* (Oxford, 1983), 367–91.

Hegel, G. W. F., *Philosophy of Right*, trans. Knox, T. M. (Oxford, 1942).

Hogan, T. Brian, *Criminal Liability Without Fault*, An Inaugural Lecture (Cambridge, 1969).

Honderich, Ted, 'On Justifying Protective Punishment', *British Journal of Criminology*, 22 (1982), 268–75.
—— *Punishment, The Supposed Justifications* (Harmondsworth, 1984).
Jacobs, Francis G., *Criminal Responsibility* (London, 1971).
Kant, Immanuel, *The Metaphysical Elements of Justice*, trans. John Ladd (Indiannapolis, 1965).
Kenny, Anthony, *Freewill and Responsibility* (London, 1978).
—— 'The Expert in Court', *The Law Quarterly Review*, 99 (1983), 197–216.
Kleinig, John, *Punishment and Desert* (The Hague, 1973).
Lacey, Nicola, 'Dangerousness and Criminal Justice: The Justification of Preventive Detention', *Current Legal Problems* (1983), 31–49.
Lyons, David, *Forms and Limits of Utilitarianism* (Oxford, 1965).
Martinson, Robert, 'New Findings, New Views: A Note of Caution Regarding Sentencing Reform', *Hofstra Law Review*, 7 (1979), 243–58.
Masters, Brian, *Killing for Company: the Case of Dennis Nilsen* (London, 1985).
McCloskey, H. J., 'The Complexity of the Concepts of Punishment', *Philosophy*, 37 (1962), 307–25.
—— 'A Non-Utilitarian Approach to Punishment', in Bayles, Michael D. (ed.), *Contemporary Utilitarianism* (New York, 1968), 239–59.
—— 'Utilitarian and Retributive Punishment', *The Journal of Philosophy*, 64 (1967), 91–110.
Mill, John Stuart, *On Liberty* in *Utilitarianism, Liberty, Representative Government*, Everyman edn. (London, 1910).
Moore, Mark H., Estrich, Susan R., McGillis, Daniel and Spelman, William, *Dangerous Offenders: The Elusive Target of Justice* (Cambridge, 1984).
Moore, Michael S., *Law and Psychiatry* (Cambridge, 1984).
Morris, Herbert, 'Persons and Punishment', in Murphy, Jeffrie G. (ed.), *Punishment and Rehabilitation* (Belmont, 1973), 40–64.
—— 'A Paternalistic Theory of Punishment', in Sartorius, Rolf (ed.), *Paternalism* (Minneapolis, 1983), 139–52.
Morris, Norval, *The Future of Imprisonment* (Chicago & London, 1974).
—— *Madness and the Criminal Law* (Chicago & London, 1982).
Mundle, C. W. K., 'Punishment and Desert', in Acton, H. B. (ed.), *The Philosophy of Punishment* (London, 1969), 65–82.
Murphy, Jeffrie G., (ed.), *Punishment and Rehabilitation* (Belmont, 1973).
—— *Retribution, Justice, and Therapy* (Dordrecht, 1979).
—— 'Retributivism and the State's Interest in Punishment', in Pen-

nock, J. R. and Chapman, J. (eds), *Nomos XXVII: Criminal Justice* (New York, 1985), 156–64.

Nagin, Daniel, 'General Deterrence: A Review of the Empirical Evidence', in Blumstein, A., Cohen, J., and Daniel, N. (eds), *Deterrence and Incapacitation: Estimating the Effects of Criminal Sanctions on Crime Rates* (Washington, 1978), 95–139.

Nathanson, Stephen, 'Does It Matter If the Death Penalty Is Arbitrarily Administered?', *Philosophy & Public Affairs*, 14 (1985), 149–64.

Nielsen, Kai, 'Against Moral Conservatism', in Struhl, Karsten J., and Struhl, Paula Rothenberg (eds), *Ethics in Perspective* (New York, 1975), 113–24. Reprinted from *Ethics*, 82 (1971–2), 219–31.

Nozick, Robert, *Anarchy, State and Utopia* (Oxford, 1974).

—— *Philosophical Explanations* (Oxford, 1981).

Parent, W. A., 'The Whole Life View of Criminal Desert', *Ethics*, 86 (1976), 350–4.

Pennock, J. R. and Chapman, J. (eds), *Nomos XXVII: Criminal Justice* (New York, 1985).

Potas, Ivan, *Just Deserts for the Mad* (Canberra, 1982).

Primorac, Igor, 'Is Retributivism Analytic?', *Philosophy*, 56 (1981), 203–11.

Quinton, Anthony M., 'On Punishment', in Acton, H. B., (ed.), *The Philosophy of Punishment* (London, 1969), 55–64.

—— 'Views', *The Listener* (2 December 1971), 757–8.

Rawls, John, 'Two Concepts of Rules', in Acton, H. B., (ed.), *The Philosophy of Punishment* (London, 1969), 105–14.

—— *A Theory of Justice* (Oxford, 1972).

Reiman, Jeffrey H., 'Justice, Civilization, and the Death Penalty: Answering van den Haag', *Philosophy & Public Affairs*, 14 (1985), 115–48.

Report of the Committee on Mentally Abnormal Offenders (The Butler Report), HMSO Cmnd. 6244 (London, 1975).

Richards, David A. J., *The Moral Criticism of Law* (Encino & Belmont, 1977).

Schoeman, Ferdinand D., 'On Incapacitating the Dangerous', in Gross, Hyman and von Hirsch, Andrew (eds), *Sentencing* (New York, 1981), 175–86.

Sedgwick, Peter, 'Antipsychiatry from the Sixties to the Eighties', in Gove, Walter R., (ed.), *Deviance and Mental Illness (Beverly Hills, 1982), 199–223.

—— *Psycho Politics* (London, 1982).

Sherman, Michael, and Hawkins, Gordon, *Imprisonment in America* (Chicago & London, 1981).

Simmons, A. John, *Moral Principles and Political Obligations* (Princeton, 1981).

Smart, J. J. C., 'Extreme and Restricted Utilitarianism', in Bayles, Michael D. (ed.), *Contemporary Utilitarianism* (New York, 1968), 99–115.

Smart, J. J. C., and Williams, Bernard, *Utilitarianism: For and Against* (Cambridge, 1973).

Sprigge, T. L. S., 'A Utilitarian Reply to Dr. McCloskey', in Bayles, Michael D. (ed.), *Contemporary Utilitarianism* (New York, 1968), 261–99.

—— 'Punishment and Moral Responsibility', in Goldinger, Milton, (ed.), *Punishment and Human Rights* (Cambridge, 1974), 73–97.

Stevenson, Leslie, 'Mind, Brain and Mental Illness', *Philosophy*, 52 (1977), 27–43.

Szasz, Thomas, 'The Myth of Mental Illness', in Murphy, Jeffrie G., (ed.), *Punishment and Rehabilitation* (Belmont, 1973), 186–97.

Ten, C. L., *Mill on Liberty* (Oxford, 1980).

The Times (5 June 1985).

Thomas, D. A., *Principles of Sentencing*, Second edn., (London, 1982).

Thompson, D. F., 'Retribution and the Distribution of Punishment', *The Philosophical Quarterly*, 16 (1966), 59–63.

Thornton, M. T., 'Rape and Mens Rea', in Nielsen, Kai and Patten, Steven C. (eds), *New Essays in Ethics and Public Policy, Canadian Journal of Philosophy*, Supplementary Vol. 8 (1982), 119–46.

Tullock, Gordon, 'Does Punishment Deter Crime?', *The Public Interest* (1974), 103–11.

van den Haag, Ernest, *Punishing Criminals* (New York, 1975).

—— 'Refuting Reiman and Nathanson', *Philosophy & Public Affairs*, 14 (1985), 165–76.

von Hirsch, Andrew, 'Proportionality and Desert: A Reply to Bedau', *The Journal of Philosophy*, 75 (1978), 622–4.

—— 'Prediction of Criminal Conduct and Preventive Confinement of Convicted Persons', in Gross, Hyman and von Hirsch, Andrew (eds), *Sentencing* (New York, 1981), 148–74.

—— 'Doing Justice: The Principle of Commensurate Deserts', in Gross, Hyman and von Hirsch, Andrew (eds), *Sentencing* (New York & Oxford, 1981), 243–56.

Waldron, Jeremy, 'Critical Notice of Hart's *Essays in Jurisprudence and Philosophy*' *Mind*, 94 (1985), 281–96.

Walker, Nigel, *Punishment, Danger and Stigma* (Oxford, 1980).

—— 'Unscientific, Unwise, Unprofitable or Unjust?', *British Journal of Criminology*, 22 (1982), 276–84.

Wasserstrom, Richard, A., 'Strict Liability in the Criminal Law', *Stanford Law Review*, 12 (1959–60), 731–45.
—— 'H. L. A. Hart and the Doctrines of *Mens Rea* and Criminal Responsibility', *The University of Chicago Law Review*, 35 (1967), 92–126.
—— 'Retributivism and the Concept of Punishment', *The Journal of Philosophy*, 75 (1978), 620–2.
—— 'Some Problems in the Definition and Justification of Punishment', in Goldman, A. I. and Kim, J. (eds), *Values and Morals* (Dordrecht & Boston, 1978), 299–315.
—— 'Capital Punishment as Punishment: Some Theoretical Issues and Objections', *Midwest Studies in Philosophy*, 7 (1982), 473–502.
Williams, Bernard, *Ethics and the Limits of Philosophy* (London, 1985).
Wootton, Barbara, *Crime and Penal Policy* (London, 1978).
—— *Crime and the Criminal Law*, Second edn., (London, 1981).

INDEX

absolute liability *see* strict liability
absolutism 21–2, 33, 62, 75, 83
Andenaes, Johannes 9–10
annulment 38–41
Anscombe, G. E. M. 19
Armstrong, K. G. 76 n., 141
Arneson, R. J. 56 n.
Ashworth, Andrew 149–50, 155–8, 161 n.
Austin, J. L. 95 n.

Bayles, Michael D. 96–7
Bedau, Hugo Adam 156 n., 161 n.
Benn, Stanley I. 42 n., 142–3, 147 n.
Bentham, Jeremy 3, 87–9, 143–6, 148, 154
Blackstone, W. 151–2
Bottoms, A. E. 134 n., 137 n.
Brownsword, Roger 134 n., 137 n.
Burgh, Richard W. 57–8, 63, 94
Butler Report 126, 130

capital punishment *see* death penalty
Cohen, Jacqueline 12
compensation 38–9, 55
consequentialist 3, 21–3, 44, 60, 75 n., 146
Cooper, David E. 39–42
Cottingham, John 51 n., 52 n., 75 n.
Cross, Sir Rupert 156 n., 161 n.
culpability 6, 46, 97, 100 n., 105, 112, 119, 146–7, 154–7
Curley, E. M. 104 n.

dangerousness 12, 134–40, 162
death penalty 41, 75, 141–2, 151–2
debt 49, 54
Dennett, Daniel C. 91 n.
Denning, Lord 41–2
denunciation 40–2
desert 5, 46–65, 67, 71, 95–6, 97, 118, 138–9, 150–60, 164
determinism 91, 113
deterrent effects of punishment 7, 9–13, 37, 45–6, 60, 87, 91, 112, 120–1, 141–2, 144–5, 147–8, 162, 164
diminished responsibility 123, 128–30, 133

distributive justice 5, 35, 47, 64, 71 n., 93, 136–40
Dixon, Chief Justice 125
Dworkin, Ronald 22, 91 n., 99–100

equivalence between crime and punishment 153–4, 159
excuses 5–6, 46, 53, 81, 82, 85, 86–100, 118–21, 123, 126–7, 130–3
Ezorsky, Gertrude 49, 91, 106–10, 114

fairness 5, 49–65, 83, 105–9, 118–21
    principle of fairness or fair play 55–7, 82–3
fantastic examples and situations 14, 18–32, 34–5
Feinberg, Joel 3 n., 16 n., 109 n., 117 n., 130 n.
fines 15–16, 109, 122
Fingarette, Herbert 124 n., 125 n., 126
Finnis, John 53, 55, 59–60, 63
Fletcher, George 87 n., 95 n., 96
Flew, A. G. N. 2–3 n., 77–8
Floud, Jean *see* Floud Report
Floud Report 134–7, 140
Forst, Martin L. 161 n.
Fuller, Lon L. 113–14
fundamental or ultimate moral principle 20–5, 27–32

Galligan, D. J. 54, 59, 161 n.
Gauthier, David P. 73 n.
Gibbs, Jack P. 6 n.
Gross, Hyman 100 n., 127, 147 n., 161 n.

Hadfield, J. 124–5
Hampshire, Stuart 30 n., 32 n.
Hampton, Jean 7–8 n.
Hare, R. M. 27–32, 36
Harris, John 156 n., 158 n.
Hart, H. L. A. 3 n., 15–16, 35 n., 41–2, 55, 62–3, 65 n., 81–5, 86–100, 101–5, 115, 116 n., 118, 121, 130 n., 143 n., 148–9, 152 n., 154 n., 158 n.
Hawkins, Gordon 163
Hegel, G. W. F. 38–41
Hinckley, J. 123

Hogan, T. Brian 100 n.
Honderich, Ted 46 n., 51 n., 52 n., 134 n., 137 n., 143 n., 147 n.

incapacitative effect of punishment 8–9, 12–13, 37, 162–3
insanity 87, 91, 119, 121, 123–34, 147; *see also* mental illness
intuitions 14, 27–32, 47–8
irresistible impulse 125, 127–33

Jacobs, Francis G. 113–15
justification (distinguished from excuse) 95–6

Kant, Immanuel 75
Kenny, Anthony 104–5 n., 124 n., 127, 132, 133 n.
King George III 124–5
Kleinig, John 47–8, 151, 152 n., 153 n.

Lacey, Nicola 137 n.
lex talionis 151–3, 154, 159
Lyons, David 69 n.

McCloskey, H. J. 13, 15
McNaghten, Daniel 124–5; *see also* McNaghten Rules
McNaghten Rules 123–7, 130–3
Martinson, Robert 160 n.
Masters, Brian 129 n.
medical treatment (distinguished from punishment) 15
mens rea 100–22, 130–1, 156
mental illness, 6, 93, 115–16, 123–40; *see also* insanity
mentally abnormal *see* mental illness
Mill, John Stuart 74
mitigation 97, 120, 133–4, 140, 144, 146–50, 152, 161, 162
Moore, Mark H. 12 n., 134 n., 136 n., 139 n.
Moore, Michael S. 131 n.
Morgan rape case 104–5, 157
Morris, Herbert 52–65, 73–4, 98
Morris, Norval 133 n., 135, 162
Mundle, C. W. K. 72, 77, 141 n.
Murphy, Jeffrie G. 48 n., 53, 55, 63–4

Nagin, Daniel 9
natural law
  minimum content of 62–3

Nazi war criminal 47–52, 79–80
necessary condition 40, 66–7, 75–9, 96 n., 102 n.
negligence 100–5, 111, 115, 121–2, 154–5, 157
Nielsen, Kai 19 n., 21
Nilsen, Dennis 129
Nozick, Robert 42–6, 56–7, 61–2, 91 n., 95–7

objective test of liability 101–5
obligation 55–7, 72–3
offence 2, 15–16

Panel on Research on Deterrent and Incapacitative Effects 9–12
Parent, W. A. 49
Peel, Sir Robert 124
Potas, Ivan 125 n., 131 n., 133 n.
proportionality 58, 141–50, 154–60, 161–2
provocation 147–50
punishment
  defining features of 2, 14–17, 42, 109, 119
  exemplary 35, 120, 143–5, 159
  main theories of 3–5
  of the innocent 4, 13–37, 60–2, 65, 67, 68–71, 77–81, 82, 83, 93
  pluralist approach to 6, 59, 77–85

quarantine 14–15, 83, 119, 121, 138
Quinton, Anthony M. 14–17, 32–4

Rawls, John 55, 67–71, 82
Reagan, President Ronald 123
recidivism 9–10, 12–13, 44, 112–13, 118, 120, 137
recklessness 101, 104, 122, 154–6
reformative effect of punishment 7–8, 9, 44–6, 141–2, 160
rehabilitative effect of punishment *see* reformative effect of punishment
Reiman, Jeffrie H. 152 n.
responsibility 33–4, 88–90, 95–6, 112–14, 126–34
retributivism 4–5, 38–65, 66–7, 68, 71–85, 94–8, 118, 139, 150–60, 161–2
revenge 43, 47, 51, 64, 150, 153
Richards, David A. J. 36, 124 n.
rights 39–41, 61–2, 76

Schoeman, Ferdinand D. 140 n.

Sedgwick, Peter 129 n., 131 n.
sentencing 6, 112, 116–17, 133–40, 146–7, 156–8, 160–4
  protective 6, 134–40
Sherman, Michael 163
side-constraints (and constraints) 61–2, 76, 83–5, 92, 94, 118, 152, 159
Simmons, A. John 56 n.
Smart, J. J. C. 4 n., 69 n.
Sprigge, T. L. S. 18 n., 24–7, 88–90
State's function 48, 74, 78
Stephen, James Fitzjames 51–2
Stevenson, Leslie 131 n.
strict liability 86, 88, 91, 92–3, 100, 105–22
subjective test of liability 101–5
subordinate or secondary moral principle 20–1, 25, 27–32
sufficient condition 40, 66–7, 75–9, 91, 96 n., 102 n.
Sutcliffe, P. W. 129
Szasz, Thomas 131 n.

tax (distinguished from punishment) 15–16, 55, 122
'telishment' 68–71

temptation 147–50
Ten, C. L. 4 n., 48 n., 52 n., 74 n.
The Times 163 n.
Thomas, D. A. 135, 144, 145 n., 146 n.
Thornton, M. T. 103–5
torture 32–6, 152, 154
treatment 6, 93, 110–22
Tullock, Gordon 10

utilitarianism 3, 7–37, 47–8, 50–1, 52, 60, 61, 65, 66–71, 72–3, 78–85, 87–94, 110, 114, 135–7, 141–50, 153, 159–62

van den Haag, Ernest 138, 152 n., 153 n.
victims 38–9, 43, 44, 47, 49–50, 55, 64, 68, 91, 93, 108–10, 136–9, 151–3
von Hirsch, Andrew 140 n., 156 n., 161 n.

Waldron, Jeremy 158 n.
Walker, Nigel 12, 41 n., 134 n., 136, 138 n.
Wasserstrom, Richard A. 3 n., 15, 55 n., 102 n, 106–8, 117 n., 119 n.
Williams, Bernard 4 n., 28 n., 31 n.
Wootton, Lady Barbara 5–6, 86, 110–22, 123, 127, 128–34